Praise for
You're in the Right Place

"Colette Baron-Reid takes us on a brilliant journey through the uncharted world of consciousness where the real magic happens. As she masterfully balances age-old wisdom with practical tools and guidance, you'll see that change isn't so difficult or scary after all. A must-read for any soul on the self-evolving journey back home."

— **Dr. Joe Dispenza**, *New York Times* best-selling author of *You Are the Placebo*

"Are you ready to go someplace you've never been? Through an inspired process of practical soul work—tools you can really use—this book will light up the dark places in your life and show you they aren't so dark at all: they're full of beauty, possibility, and fun."

— **Kris Carr**, *New York Times* best-selling author

"Your soul is calling you! Your life adventure can't start without you. Now is the time to follow the holy plan for your life. Be sure to take this brilliant new book with you for travel reading. Thank you, Colette, for your loving and delightful soul guidance."

— **Robert Holden**, author of *Shift Happens!* and *Life Loves You*

"Colette Baron-Reid is a rare and wonderful hybrid: she is both a wise teacher and a Harley-riding modern-day mystic who authentically shares her path to transformation. Don't miss the opportunity to learn from her."

— **Arielle Ford**, author of *Turn Your Mate into Your Soulmate*

"A magnificent, magical, and super-practical guide to your interior landscape, from the peaks of your inner mountaintops to the depths of your ocean floor. Let Colette expertly support you, with her signature style of exercises and inquiry, to excavate your own unknown territories and realms so the best and brilliant you can emerge."

— **Nancy Levin**, author of *Worthy*

"I knew the first time I talked to Colette that she and I were headed for big things. Not only is she brilliant, wise, and wholeheartedly connected to magic, but she knows, like few others, that spirituality is meant to be fun. Who else would call the bigger thing Quantum Fred, a title I delight in every time she playfully mentions it? Colette is privy to the fact that taking ourselves less seriously and playing around in the infinite field of possibility is the only real way to experience Truth. In this remarkable new book, she joins forces with Fred to deliver brand-new revelations. Pump your fists in the air, as I did when I read this book, and know you're about to embark on the journey of a lifetime."

— **Pam Grout**, *New York Times* best-selling author of *E-Squared*

"This book is an enlightening and intimate look into the process of self-discovery and destiny co-creation. In her fun and inimitable style, Colette Baron-Reid offers practical yet life-changing techniques in the perfect combination of the light-hearted and the profound. This book can help you tap your most powerful source of all solutions, the Realm of Spirit—not just a new-age concept here but a very real presence of support. Open the pages and you'll soon find your life moving in new directions, sailing into a future filled with love, adventure, and unlimited possibilities!"

— **Sandra Anne Taylor**, *New York Times* best-selling author of *Quantum Success* and *Your Quantum Breakthrough*

"Colette Baron-Reid beautifully guides you on a personal journey beyond your limitations to experience your potential in a way you might have never thought possible! Fantastic book!"

— **John Holland**, medium and best-selling author of *Born Knowing* and *Power of the Soul*

"A fascinating and uplifting voyage through our interdimensional soul. This book empowers you to boldly navigate the unpredictable seas of existence and unearth the lustrous pearls hidden in life's unfolding . . . and it's so fun. If you're ready for a true sea change in your life, get this book."

— **Jennifer McLean**, creator of Healing with the Masters and author of *Spontaneous Transformation*

You're in the Right Place

Other Hay House Products by Colette Baron-Reid

Books

The Map

Messages from Spirit

The Oracle Card Journal

Oracle of the 7 Energies Journal

Remembering the Future

Card Decks

Crystal Spirits Oracle

The Dream Weaver's Oracle

The Enchanted Map Oracle Cards

Goddess Power Oracle Cards

The Good Tarot

Guides of the Hidden Realms Oracle

Mystical Shaman Oracle (with Alberto Villoldo and Marcela Lobos)

The Oracle of E (with Pam Grout)

Oracle of the 7 Energies

Postcards from Spirit

The Shaman's Dream Oracle (with Alberto Villoldo)

The Spirit Animal Oracle

The Wisdom of Avalon Oracle Cards

Wisdom of the Hidden Realms Oracle Cards

Wisdom of the Oracle Divination Cards

You're in the Right Place

Let Go of the Past, Make Friends with Uncertainty, and Discover the Magic of an Uncharted Future

COLETTE BARON-REID

HAY HOUSE INDIA
New Delhi • London • Sydney
Carlsbad, California • New York City

Hay House Publishers (India) Pvt Ltd
Muskaan Complex, Plot No. 3, B-2, Vasant Kunj, New Delhi - 110070, India

Hay House LLC, P.O. Box 5100, Carlsbad, CA 92018-5100, USA
Hay House UK Ltd, 1st Floor, Crawford Corner, 91-93 Baker Street, London W1U 6QQ, UK
Hay House Australia Publishing Pty Ltd, 18/36 Ralph St., Alexandria NSW 2015, Australia

Email: contact@hayhouse.co.in
Website: www.hayhouse.co.in

Cover design: Jordan Wannemacher • ***Interior design:*** Nick C. Welch

This book was previously published through Hay House as *Uncharted: The Journey Through Uncertainty to Infinite Possibility*.

First published by Hay House India, 2025
10 9 8 7 6 5 4 3 2 1

ISBN 978-93-6611-122-3

Printed at Repro India Limited

MIX
Paper from responsible sources
FSC www.fsc.org FSC® C047271

Hay House is committed to a sustainable future for our business, our readers and our planet. This book is made from Forest Stewardship Council® certified paper.

For Marc—
I stepped into the Unknown
with you and found magic.

CONTENTS

PREFACE TO THE NEW EDITION

In the 36-plus years that I've been working in the intuitive arts and personal transformation field, I've witnessed the intricacies behind people's stories, including their motivations, unseen patterns, hidden agendas, and ancestral legacy. This is how I came to my understanding of the Map of your life as the way to understanding and transforming yourself and claiming your inherent magic.

Inside all of us are psychospiritual landscapes created by our thoughts, feelings, beliefs, memories, and intentions. Through Mapmaking, we understand our lives as a journey through these places. Instead of a paper map showing physical destinations, you explore a Map of your soul. When you can see where you have been and how you got to where you were, the story of your life takes on greater depth and meaning. You see the connecting elements of fate and destiny in what appeared to be unrelated experiences. Through symbolic language, we move beyond the surface of things to access the layers of experience that are stored in our subconscious minds and are often hidden from our everyday awareness.

In 2010, I published my best-selling book *The Map,* which introduced people to the concept of the Map and my Invision Process—since renamed The Total Mindshift Process®. I then felt called to write *Uncharted,* now updated and re-released almost a decade later as *You're in the Right Place.* (Don't worry if you haven't read either book! This book will stand on its own.)

In this book, you will learn what to do when the old Map of your life stops being useful and you find yourself in unfamiliar experiences in the uncharted places. In times of uncertainty, chaos, emotional turbulence, and total freak-outs, your natural instinct is to run away, but you must resist. When you accept the unlimited abundance of the Universe and the infinite possibilities for your life, it becomes clearer to see that no matter what is going on, you are in the right place. If you start to explore where you are, the magic of alchemy can happen. All that you need, all the answers you seek, are here, inside you, not somewhere out there.

In the uncharted, there is powerful magic that can help you transform your life in ways you might never have imagined. But before we can take that first step, there's an important introduction that needs to be made. . . .

A TV SHOW AND A CHANNEL

In September 2014, before I'd even started writing this book, I taped a national Canadian television show in Toronto for MZTV called *Messages from Spirit with Colette Baron-Reid*, in which I did readings as an intuitive counselor and medium. Over the course of three weeks and during 12 shooting days, I brought through approximately 300 spontaneous readings for audience members (and for crew members too, much to their surprise). It was a marathon! I had never experienced anything like this. Seriously, when the dead insist on using you as their mouthpiece, saying no is not really an option—but more about that later.

The energy of the experience didn't leave me once I left the TV studio. I just wasn't the same going out as I was when I went in. And surprisingly the spirits did not drift away as I had expected. Instead it was as if they remained with me, and for a long while I felt their presence no matter where I was.

Although the individual readings had been detailed and personal, the messages I was now receiving were much more than a collection of apologies, requests for forgiveness, declarations of love, and sweet reconciliations. Together, the spirits constituted an overarching energy that was like a flock of birds flying in unison, communicating as one, moving in one large mass of connected light and energy. And in the months that followed the show's taping, I began to notice a lingering "they" that were different from a group of dead people, like unexpected guests at a party who came through the same door and never left. "They" were still somehow gathered at the outer edges of my awareness.

During the show taping, doing all those readings, I was aware that I was tuning in to individual personalities that showed up to reveal aspects of who they "were" in order to contact their living loved ones. But at the same time, I was tuning in to something else now, some other intelligence that suddenly was present too—a collective source of loving intelligence available for communication.

Up to this point, while receiving messages, I had received details about people who had crossed over, and about events that had occurred in their lives, in several ways: feeling the messages emotionally and energetically as sensations (clairsentience), hearing words or sounds (clairaudience), or having inner "knowings" that came from the spirits (claircognizance). To me and to the person receiving the reading, it seemed perfectly obvious that I was communicating with the consciousness of an individual that retained their own unique personality traits. Now it was being made clear that a spirit retains their individual personality and memories after crossing over, but the spirits are not as separated from each other and us in the same way that individuals are separated in life.

There are other intelligences that want to help us too. We're surrounded by beings who want us to succeed and evolve both individually and collectively. We're not alone, even though we perceive separation. In fact, these spirits are intrinsically connected to all of us, and woven into a web of living Mind existing within the Mind of the Greater Consciousness called God, Spirit, Source, the Quantum Field, Divine Intelligence—there are many names, none of which can quite capture the complexity and vastness of what this really is. Generally, I'll use the term *Spirit* with a capital *S* to represent the Consciousness of the Universe, this matrix where all possibilities exist.

It took me months to process what I was experiencing, as it was impossible for me to talk about it even with other mediums. I didn't quite understand what was going on, and I was feeling almost protective of it. Meanwhile, I had begun writing this book, which I had planned to be a straightforward sequel to my book *The*

Map. Every once in a while, as I veered off into a more heady and intellectual approach to my writing, I got flooded with that same intelligent "other" energy and gently guided to new, simpler ideas and to insights that seemed to come out of nowhere. It's like "they" had the puzzle pieces, and when I was ready for them, they dropped them down on the page for me to discover. This was my first (but not last) time channeling a distinct nonhuman consciousness. It was a humbling experience, as my inner critical cynic had always doubted others when they shared their channeling stories.

Over the next several months, when I wasn't trying to overanalyze the content I was downloading, I began to trust that something important was happening to me and through me and for the benefit of others. This copilot was informing me as a Chorus of many, come together as one harmonic intelligence with words, pictures, and ideas as if I were merely a conduit. Still, they let my editor and me shape this book. We all worked together!

I'd always understood that individual consciousness is woven into a greater consciousness that is Spirit. Now, through this very active and chatty intelligence that is neither one nor many, I began truly experiencing this truth. I'm grateful for this profound gift from Spirit.

INTRODUCING . . . FRED

I'd always understood that we're supposed to be joyful and curious and remember to be playful, but the way this Chorus communicated with me drove that point home completely.

When I handed in the first draft of this section of my book to my editor, she said to me in her grounded Capricorn way, "You need to call these spirits something. I need a noun. Plural, singular, whatever. I need consistent terms."

I didn't feel that "spirits" was an accurate description of this Chorus. They weren't a bunch of disembodied spirits, plural. As weird as it might sound to you, I know the difference between dead people talking to me and this collective group. Should I simply call them the Chorus? After all, they have a singsong sound that pings in harmony when I hear them. They had the energy of a chorus of angels. . . .

"Ask them!" my editor suggested. So I went into meditation and did exactly that, and listened for an answer . . .

"We are We. You are We. We are Light. We are When You Listen."

Then I closed my eyes again and saw an image of Dana Carvey from the film *Wayne's World* with his wig and glasses on—this was not working out the way I expected it to at all. I didn't even like that movie when I saw it years ago! Was this a trick of my imagination? It sure didn't feel like it.

I asked, "Um—you guys still there?"

Buzzing happy joyful wisdom senses overload . . . (I guessed that would be a yes.)

I asked again: "I don't know what to call you."

The answer came: *"We are 'We'! Fred!"*

Then I remembered that I sometimes have playfully referred to a Higher Power, or God, as Quantum Fred. But I always did that as kind of a fun way to say Divine Intelligence or Spirit, to stay out of the religious context of referring to a Greater Consciousness. And to be honest, I sure didn't want this Chorus to be named "Fred"! As far as I knew, there were no angels named Fred. I've had to work hard on my fear of not being taken seriously, of being seen as delusional or heretical at worst, or lacking intellectual sophistication at best. At least could the name be more mythical—Raphael, or even Gandalf? Or something people would already be familiar with, that already has some clout in the collective, like Angel Gabriel?

Nope . . . I get Fred.

"Please don't tell me to call you Fred," I implored.

"Fred. Fred. Fred."

So . . . "they" are "Fred."

After my meditation and communication, I searched online for the meaning of the name Fred and discovered it meant "peaceful ruler." My best friend told me the name of the Dana Carvey character in *Wayne's World* was Garth, and further research showed me that *Garth* means "garden" and "defender," and "defender of the innocent." Another friend told me that Garth in *Wayne's World* is an innocent and a character we're meant to laugh with.

So here we have it: *Fred* is the Consciousness of Peace, the Defender of the Garden. They let me know that we are here to create and that there's always enough in the garden, and we must defend that against our fear. We have to be playful as we plant, grow, and co-create.

So, like it or not, I had to go along with calling them Fred to remind myself, and you, of their message.

The extraordinarily powerful experience of meeting Fred felt like being dunked back in the spiritual deep end. You could also say I was auto-enrolled in a crash course on humility and grace, which provided me with a newfound trust in the Invisible. What did I learn and internalize from the experience? That our challenge is to let go of our old stories that defined us and forgive others *and* ourselves. Dropping those stories will free us from the burdens and restrictions that have prevented us from writing new ones.

Fred taught me to get past my ego's fear of not being credible enough. Make no mistake about it: Talking about self-evolution and what we are going to co-create for ourselves is very serious business. But we're meant to wear the world loosely around our shoulders, drop our masks, and relax and play. So as you read this book, I want you to keep that in mind and remember to lighten up. Take time away to be in the joy and silliness of life too, because self-evolution is hard work.

INTRODUCTION

It's time to wake up.

We are spiritual beings constrained by our human experience, asleep at the wheel of life. We're in a state of spiritual amnesia, having forgotten our purpose and seeing only through a distorted lens of perception and perspective that accepts a finite and limited universe.

So many of us are hearing a calling from the soul at this time of tremendous global change, when we're being pressured to evolve into who we have to be to have the experiences we want to co-create. Any illusion that we could keep going the way we were is nearly impossible to sustain now. The urge to change from caterpillar to butterfly is simply too strong.

My own discomfort at how I've defined my own journey has been forcing me to strip away more and more layers that no longer serve. Many of you are feeling that too.

It's time for us to stop trying to duct-tape together what's broken and instead co-create something new.

It's time for us to look beyond the map of the familiar and sail into uncharted waters.

This is the epiphany, the gift, from those who have crossed over to the realm beyond the veil: We don't have to carry around the pain, the shame, or the belief that somehow what happened to us was our fault or that we are unworthy of what we desire—love, joy, acceptance, expression, and belonging. We are powerful co-creators with Spirit. We no longer have to go by the old, familiar maps that were etched into being by those experiences.

When we're lost, we all want a map—but maps can only tell us where we've been. They can only reflect the past and our memories of experiences. But we are headed into the uncharted places, into an unknown future that has not yet been imagined.

Where are *you* going? What do *you* want to co-create?

With the help of Spirit, we can co-create anything we want—but what we create will fade away like a mirage if we don't evolve into the people we need to be. What our lives will look like isn't the point. What form our relationships, careers, or abundance take is immaterial. Where we'll live, how we'll communicate, how we'll get along with the other people in our lives—there are infinite possibilities for what we could bring about into our physical reality in the Realm of Form. But we have to believe that we can, with Spirit's help, handle the awesome power of co-creation and not slip back into the old, fear-driven ways of operating that got us to where we are now. We're afraid we don't have what it takes to handle the responsibility that comes with the power of co-creativity, but with the guidance of Spirit and working together with others, we can learn to trust ourselves—and we can co-create responsibly. The old story that someone has to bail us out or save us can be replaced.

All of us have to create and be re-created again and again so that we can experience what our soul came here to experience and bring into being the world we desire.

Each of us is undergoing a transformation as we enter the Age of Consciousness. Your life can't remain exactly as it is, but that's okay, because you can *consciously* participate in this evolution with awareness. You aren't a victim of the change. You can make your personal transformation not just one that fulfills you and gives you a sense of purpose and meaning, but one that ends up contributing to the well-being of all.

Yes, your conscious choice to evolve is that important. It may not be curing cancer or healing all the suffering in the world, but believe me, it's important. Your personal evolution will not only inspire others but help in raising the vibration and consciousness of everyone around the globe.

YOU'RE IN THE RIGHT PLACE

So what does this mean for your little corner of the world—your life and your challenges? I have always said that I'm not just an intuitive counselor or coach or medium but a spiritual cartographer. I can help you orient yourself so that you're not paralyzed with fear and uncertainty. I want to help you hear your soul's calling, find the courage to co-create something new, which is the magical promise of journeying into the uncharted. Where are you? Where do you want to be? Who do you need to become? These are the questions you will explore as you work with this book.

I will help you understand and use the multidimensional Map of your soul, which you can only see when the spiritual amnesia lifts and you step into the Realm of Spirit. It is in this realm that you recognize you are an eternal soul always connected to the divine creative force. It is here where you feel at home, you recognize that you have underestimated your potential, and you begin a process of personal evolution that can help you to face whatever challenges appear.

What will you learn from this book that will help you in your everyday life to break out of old patterns?

I'll teach you:

- How to manage your fear and discomfort and "train your dragons" (that is, own and wisely use your personal power)
- How to tune in to that powerful co-creative zone where miracles wait to be discovered
- How to let go of your limited ideas of who you are and who you might become, and the old stories that have confined you
- What tools you can use to help you remain conscious of your authentic nature as a spiritual being always connected to, supported by, and loved by Spirit
- How to journey through the five interconnected realms where you will actually do the work of co-creating what you want to experience
- How self-evolution can help you to co-create what you desire—and sustain it

You are about to journey far beyond where you have gone before and follow the dictates of your soul instead of the dictates of your fear. If the old ways aren't working for you anymore, you've come to the right place.

When you remember who you truly are, magic happens. You step into your role as a co-creator—and I do mean *co*-creator. As Joseph Campbell said, if you take just one step toward the gods, the gods will take ten steps toward you. Life will get much easier when you take that first step toward Spirit and plunge into the uncharted, unfamiliar places of self-discovery, and access the magic there.

So first, you'll learn more about the Map of your soul, how to access it, and the journey you'll take from what you know to what you haven't yet discovered. You'll also learn how to find your courage and unleash your personal power so you can evolve and co-create something new. That's Part I of this book. Then, in Part II, with your soul's Map to guide you, you will make a metaphorical journey through five interconnected realms. The first is the Realm of Spirit, where everything possible exists in the invisible and where you remember and experience your spiritual nature, which then leads you to four more realms: the Realm of Mind, where you experience consciousness; the Realm of Light, where you illuminate the darkness, reclaim lost parts of yourself, and discover the spark of transformation; the Realm of Energy, where you work with the forces influencing you and experience transformation within; and the Realm of Form, where you experience your transformation reflected in matter as you make changes in your life with the support of Spirit.

Finally, in the last chapter of this book, you will come to understand the revolution in consciousness we're all experiencing and how you can participate in it to contribute to the world in your own unique way—even as you embark on your own personal journey of transformation.

Throughout the book you'll find exercises drawn from the Total Mindshift Process. Try to do these exercises in a quiet place where you will have privacy and won't be interrupted, and make sure you have pen and paper to record what you experience and your interpretation of it afterward. Even better, get a notebook and start an "uncharted" journal! If you get confused at any point, you can flip to the Glossary in the back of this book for a refresher on some key concepts and terms.

If you come with me and journey through this book, I hope you'll learn something new and be reminded about something you've always known but needed to hear again. Exploring the uncharted can be initially disorienting since they are unfamiliar and unrecognizable to the conditioned mind, but it can also be extraordinary and awe inspiring. There's so much to discover about yourself and your power to change your life.

The truth is that you will take a journey into the uncharted more than once in your life, and it will be more intense at some times than at others. You will heal more and evolve more on the journeys that are more emotionally intense and difficult, but all your journeys to the uncharted will contribute to your evolution.

Again and again, you will be pulled into this spiraling journey, whether you want to go or not! But even if you're dragged into it kicking and screaming, you will emerge stronger, wiser, happier, and with a greater sense of purpose. The pain of change is never in vain—it always leads to something better for you and for everyone you touch. The authentic, empowered you co-creates with greater love and compassion! Fred says we're here to tend and defend the garden, to plant and create, and trust that there is always enough for everyone if we garden well. Oh, and we're supposed to have fun!

Fred says: *"Remember who you were before you came to be. You have the power to write a new story for your life so you can begin to live it. Your new story becomes the new story for all."* I believe that once you start taking this journey to the uncharted, you'll see that change isn't so scary after all. It can even be exhilarating and fun. Join me, for I have all kinds of things to share to make the voyage across those waves light up, even when the swells get intense. So let this journey begin!

PART I

ORIENTING YOURSELF IN THE REALM OF SPIRIT

1

UNCHARTED WATERS AND HIDDEN MAGIC

On the uncharted areas of ancient mariners' maps, you would often see a dire warning: "There be dragons!" Sailors feared venturing forth into unknown waters lest they encounter fierce monsters. Of course, the dragons weren't real—or maybe they were, and we just haven't discovered their bones yet! However, the sailors' fear wasn't completely irrational. After all, some of those sailors did meet with tragic fates as ships were overcome by swells or wrecked by storms. Yet someone had to set sail for the lands undiscovered. If not, there would be nothing on the map!

The yearning to explore is core to our human nature. We aren't content to have everything remain the same forever. Even if we think we want that, it's not possible. Life happens, circumstances change, and we have to locate a boat and set out on a new adventure. We can't let a fear of dragons hold us back from living—but too often, we do.

Could there be dragons out there? Of course! But what if you could train the dragons and get them to be your allies? What if instead of singeing you, they used their fiery breath to light up dark places and reveal hidden treasures? What if they allowed you to climb on their backs and soar about the landscape of your life, giving you a new perspective, empowering you to let go of your old limiting patterns?

And what if avoiding the uncharted places meant you lost out on the magic of fulfillment, joy, a sense of purpose, and marvelous possibilities you haven't even imagined yet?

Yes, there be dragons there, and *there be magic too.*

When you journey into the unknown, you may indeed meet those dragons the ancient mapmakers warned of, but you can consider creating a different relationship with them. You can get to know them. If you do, you will see that what you instinctively fear is *your own power*—that's right, dragons are a symbol of your personal power. Dragons can help you trust yourself to use your co-creative powers wisely, responsibly, and joyfully as you break the rules of convention, say no to the old ways, and let go of the stories that have kept you small and frightened.

Your past has defined the Map you use to navigate your life. That's how the mind works: relying on memory to make sense of what is happening today and to plan for a tomorrow that is always uncertain. But if you're like a lot of people, you've come to recognize that no matter how much control you try to take over your own circumstances, how much pleading you do to a power greater than you, in some areas of your life it has become much harder to create what you desire when you rely on what you've known already. That old Map is not a reliable guide for a future that's uncertain and unknown.

Lots of people try to co-create what they desire by wishing, thinking, affirming what their past experience tells them they desire. They don't go deep enough into themselves to find out what they really want. They get attached to the form of abundance they think will make them feel safe—money, for example! They get attached to the form of love they think will make them feel lovable or define their worth—a romantic partner who says "I love you!" over and over or a big bank account with lots of toys and trips. Then they get confused when they do manifest what they want, and somehow it doesn't make them feel the way they thought it would. Everyone wants money and romantic love, but it's the motive driving the desire that is the real point. Why we want those things and for what end, how much attachment we have and how indentured we still are to the stories that cause us to chase results determine if we can live freely or not.

When you go deep within yourself to discover who you really are and what you desire at your very core, you get past any limited notions about what's going to give you a sense of fulfillment and purpose. You find that to co-create something truly new, you have to evolve into the person who can step into your new life with confidence and ease. There is no way to sustain the changes you manifest if you're looking for the outside to change first. You'll get stuck operating according to subconscious patterns mapped into your brain long ago. You'll become trapped in an old story about who you are that doesn't match up with what you want to experience.

What you need is a new Map that shows you how to find your way to a new you and a new life. This Map has the familiar places on it, but unfamiliar places too—the uncharted places that will only be filled in when you begin to have new experiences. And this Map is both complex and mysterious, because it is the Map of your soul. Your soul isn't looking to avoid all suffering and move straight ahead from goal to goal to goal, because it has its own agenda, one that you were born with. It's looking for experiences, and to have them, it will pull you into a journey to the uncharted more than once in this lifetime.

The journey I'm talking about isn't about a trek to undiscovered places on planet Earth, and I'm not suggesting there are literal dragons out there. I'm talking about powerful forces that exist *inside you,* waiting at the outer edges of your consciousness to claim them. These dragons need to be trained and redirected: you have to own and use your power to co-create something new for yourself—with the help and guidance of Spirit.

And the journey you will take is not a straightforward path from here to there, an adventure that takes place in the outside world where you set goals and strive to achieve them. I'm all for that kind of journey, but this one is inward, and it spirals deeper and deeper into you until you find the parts of yourself that you were afraid to face and claim before. It's a journey you can't resist, because if you do, you will soon find that your life isn't working.

You will always know there is something more that you haven't quite gotten a handle on.

We are all called into uncharted places at some point—by a failed relationship, a serious health crisis, a breakdown, a disaster, or circumstances set in motion by the people around us while we were busy over there, co-creating a nice little life for ourselves. *What happened? I had my "thing" all together, and now this?* It's at these times that we're called to evolve into the powerful, purposeful co-creators we came here to be.

Are you being pulled inward? Do you sense you need to do something bigger, make changes that are more dramatic, take your life in a whole new direction? Listen to that inner voice. It knows what you need, because it's the voice of your soul.

On this journey to the uncharted, you will be led by intuition. Many people call that the sixth sense, but I call it the *first* sense, because it's the sense of the soul—the sense that activates when you quiet the stimulation from your five senses and intellect. You have to become still and move out of self-centeredness to tune in to your intuition. Intuition is your direct line to Spirit! And on this journey, you will change from the inside out and start to see your internal changes reflected in your circumstances and in the world around you.

YOUR SOUL IS CALLING—PLEASE PICK UP!

You have, and have always had, the power to help shape the outer world and its conditions. Maybe you have co-created many wonderful situations and relationships and feel a greater sense of purpose than you ever have before. But don't you feel that it's hard to move forward as you always have because of what is going on around you in the world right now? How can we plan our individual lives when all around us we see radical transformation and feel that no one is in charge—at least, no one with a vision and the power to enact it?

There is no one leader on Earth who can fix the challenges we're facing. In the same way, there's no one outside of you who can give you the answers and foolproof plan to create all that you want in your life right now. We are the ones who will create the vision and bring into being the world we seek. And we have to do this individually, as well as with each other. The more authentic and real you're willing to become, the more you have the power to co-create a much better world not just for you but for all of us.

Something deep inside the caverns of your psyche is beginning to transform. Can you feel the magic beckon? Are you ready to reclaim, repair, and knit together all the pieces of the authentic you that were lost within when you were wounded in your past? They can serve you now, but you have to illuminate them and see them in a new light. The old stories of your life can take on new meaning. When you free yourself from their stamp on your identity, miracles can and do happen. All it takes is willingness to let go and let something new reveal itself to you. A Map is appearing for you now, and it's like a spherical, sparkling hologram, calling you to journey home to who you truly are.

Unlike maps in the modern physical world, this Map of the soul has plenty of uncharted places. And the Map itself is only revealed when you take blind steps inward, led by your first sense.

Those steps you take will lead you into the dark, mysterious world of your inner psyche, where you can come to know yourself and Spirit and experience unconditional love and acceptance. There's no reason to be afraid, because Spirit is always with you. You will know that and feel it when you say the words that bring in the magic: not "abracadabra" but "thank you." *Thank you!* This abracadabra is simple and profound. Immersing yourself in a meditation on deep, immense gratitude invokes Spirit to fill your consciousness and remind you that you are blessed to be given the gift of life—the gift of being able to co-create reality. While we always live between the pillars of what is and what might be, we reclaim our power to be the storytellers of our own lives when we connect with Spirit through gratitude.

You're not alone and it's all good. You just forgot that, and then you got in your own way, and things ended up all screwy, didn't they? No wonder you became scared and avoided the uncharted places. *I'd better play it safe. I'd better choose from what I know and what I've seen already.* How often did you let your fear tell you that?

I get it. I've been there. A never-ending expanse of uncharted waters can be scary—at least to the small self. This self, your ego, identifies with your human existence, which will ultimately end. It is almost always afraid! Your other self, your soul, has a completely different perspective because it knows it existed before your body did and will exist afterward. It has no fear of death. That makes for a very different way of looking at life on earth and what we make of our experience here! You might say your soul self has a totally different to-do list from the one the small self might develop. It most definitely has a different Map—and a sense of humor. As the old saying goes, "Man plans. God laughs."

Now, that doesn't mean that God is laughing *at* us. Divine Consciousness is *within us* and loves us. We need to remember there is a gift waiting for us: something better, something more authentic and true to who we are, something that will help us evolve, something that is ultimately good even if it appears to be a frustrating detour in our best laid plans. If we can laugh and lighten up, it becomes easier to access the hidden Map—and to remember we have a Map in the first place.

THE MAP OF THE SOUL

Your soul's Map is like a translucent globe of energy. Paths can wind through it and around its surface, and it's hard to see the patterns when you're looking at it in two dimensions, which distorts a spherical map. Two points on the surface might seem disconnected—random events or experiences you've had. Yet if the spherical Map of the soul were to light up from within, you could see the line connecting them, winding through the middle of the sphere.

So where is this Map of the soul? Right there in front of you, and all around you—but you're not conscious of it most of the time, especially when the small self is leading the way. Your soul's Map is viewable in the hidden realms of your mind and heart. You see it when you let go of your fear, anger, despair, and emotional heaviness and orient yourself in the Realm of Spirit. If you don't know how to do all that, don't worry—you will learn! Start in the right "place," the right awareness, immersing yourself in gratitude and reverence, and everything looks different.

Let's consider this starting point to get you oriented. Imagine yourself at a shopping mall, looking at the sign that says, "You are here." *Ah yes, there's the store I want to go to. It's over here. I just have to go here, then turn right, and walk that way a bit, and bingo, I'm there.* The map in the mall is a map of places known. That's fine if you are completely satisfied with your life and absolutely certain it will never change . . . Not going to happen!

If you want your fear to fade away and myriad possibilities you never considered to start revealing themselves, you need a different Map, one that shows the unknown, unexplored places. Those are the places your soul wants to go. Your soul is here to experience life, not to simply animate yet another human body going through the motions of living—eating, sleeping, working, and so on. It wants to travel to places that aren't on the familiar Map you are looking at.

Now, you might look at your familiar Map and think, *Here's where I got everything I wanted, achieved it all, reached my goals, found love, made money, and still I know there is something more . . . Did I do something wrong?* Maybe you feel called to deeper exploration of the possibilities life presents. Greater satisfaction, a deeper sense of purpose, and an awareness that you are living according to your soul's desires—all can be yours if you switch to navigating by the Map of your soul.

The map in the metaphorical mall looks very different when you come in through a different entrance; in the same way, your Map for your life that reveals your potential, power, and purpose will look very different if you start in the Realm of Spirit. There, the many dimensions reveal themselves, and the paths that took you from experience to experience make so much more sense.

The Map of your soul incorporates the more familiar Map of your life. On the Map of your soul, you still see the place where you quit that awful job, and then moved to another city, and then met that wonderful friend by "sheer dumb luck" one day when you happened to overhear a conversation in the park and asked a stranger a question. But now you also see pathways between them that you never saw before. Now the Map has shimmering strands of silver highways. How did you miss those? Because you weren't seeing your life through the eyes of your soul, which pushed you to quit the job, whispered to you, "Move to that other city," and nudged you to walk through the park that day. Your soul was jumping up and down clapping and saying, "Yes, yes, yes!" when you approached the stranger.

And look—the silver lines on the Map of your soul are throbbing with energy and life and shining brightly. There are many of them, interwoven into a multidimensional matrix, a sphere of light and energy with threads and pathways constantly moving and swirling, intersecting and transforming through experience, which in turn is interwoven with the multidimensional matrix of all life. Your soul has a distinct path—one not seen in two dimensions.

Yes, it took you to that uncharted place where you got involved in a project and made new friends, and then someone betrayed you. It was very painful, and you quit and walked away to lick your wounds; you vowed to get tough, shut down, and never let anyone in again. Your soul chose *that*? What was it thinking? You fell in love, only to have the one who meant the most to you in all the world develop a deadly disease and cross over into the other world. That was cause for your anger and suffering, and after all that unfairness, you were entitled to payback, right? Although in truth no one was going to get that close ever again, so you built some serious walls around your heart and put a padlock on the door. Could it be that your soul wanted to have that experience? Was this really the plan? Were you meant to go there, and there, and meet him, and her?

The soul is not concerned with avoiding pain at all costs. It wants to experience life, to co-create, to be joyful, to explore, and to contribute. Those silver roads represent the times when you were listening to your soul calling you—the times when you were awake, and aware of the you who exists beyond the limits and fears of the small self. Those silver roads form the spherical living Map of your soul and they are the ones that continue to pull you to the places uncharted. It's only the small self that reacts in fear and anger when things don't follow the expected path. The small self can't see what the soul sees.

THE FIRST SENSE WILL GUIDE YOU

You are aware of the world of the five senses: hearing, sight, smell, taste, and touch (although some would say there are internal senses too—your proprioceptive sense of body awareness and your vestibular sense of movement). Your soul has access to that information too—because it is always connected to your personality or small self that is focused on what is happening in your everyday life. (You'll learn more about the small self and the soul in Chapter 2.) But your soul has another sense, intuition. And that's the one that you'll need if you want to use the Map of your soul and navigate the unfamiliar places on your soul's Map.

Your first sense, intuition, is what will help quiet your fear of uncertainty when you're feeling lost. Think of it as the power that runs your GPS app or lights up your Map of the soul. It is your connection to the hidden wisdom of Spirit.

We typically have referred to intuition as the sixth sense, but it's only "the other one" relative to the five physical senses when you look at it from the perspective of the small self (also known as the ego). The small self is unaware of all that your soul knows and can't access the knowledge and powers your soul can. I invite you again to think of this soul sense as the *first* sense instead of the sixth. The world is magical, separation is illusion, and you need this primary sense to navigate uncharted waters.

Using intuition, you can identify alternate routes and ways around or through or over obstacles. Intuition helps you decide what actions to take to fulfill the longings of your soul, because it lets you access the soul's Map and see its multidimensional intricacies. In fact, intuition gives you direct communication with Spirit, which you need more than ever when faced with uncertainty. You can use prayer to ask Spirit for help, but using intuition helps you to take in and understand Spirit's response when you pray. Intuition is a tool for dialogue.

Your intuition is always there for you, but like a muscle, it can atrophy if you don't use it. Too often, intuition has been written of as an odd, spooky thing not to be taken seriously—or worse, it has been condemned by those who don't understand it is a gift from Spirit that we all have. Spirit wants you to check in, dialogue, and listen, not just on rare occasions when you're really scared or upset, and not only within the construct of religion. There are many paths to enlightenment and self-realization. Pick one or pick three—just do "the 'do' things," the small things, and make those habits part of your everyday life. Pray, meditate, or use other spiritual practices, and also consider working with tools such as oracle card decks, which are like turning on your mobile device to access the GPS function—your intuition.

All oracles are indicators of the dominant and subtle energies that are flowing through your story, affecting your life. Later in the book, you'll learn more about directing these energies and about using oracles, including ones found in nature, to dialogue with Spirit and remind yourself that you're never alone. When you're in a place that's uncharted and you're scared, dialogue with Spirit. Phone home! Call your mother! Check your soul's Map and you'll see that you're okay after all.

LIGHTEN UP AND HAVE FUN!

Working with the Map of your soul, dialoguing with Spirit, and journeying into the uncharted shouldn't just be scary—it should be like an adventure, unnerving at times but thrilling too. It's like one of those virtual games you play on a mobile device or computer. You work hard to break through to the next level of play, not knowing exactly what that level will be like. You earn points and talismans that can serve you in the future as you work your way to the next spot on the Map. Some levels are harder to conquer than others. You can linger for a while on a lower level, enjoying your mastery and resting for a time before moving forward. But soon you'll grow restless and get back into the game. By recognizing that it is a game, you can start to lighten up.

I know life can feel very serious sometimes, and I don't want to minimize how hard it can be. Some people have genuine threats to their physical safety they must face. But clinging to the familiar habits to ensure safety and certainty prevents you from being present to the power available to you in moment. It snaps you back onto the two-dimensional, familiar map.

Creativity and resilience can be found here in the now as you work with the Map of your soul, and that's important, because you can't avoid the uncharted places—and anyway, you wouldn't want to miss out on the magic!

So let's get started with understanding how to work with this Map of the soul, starting in the Realm of Spirit, where you have to go to remember your true nature. It is a place of tranquility and joy, a home base that you can return to anytime you get scared or upset. It is where you can fully access your ability to observe what is happening to you rather than feeling completely immersed in it, unable to see anything but the drama of the landscape you are in.

Traveler's Notes

- To fulfill your potential, you are called into the unknown—to sail into uncharted waters where you feel uncertain. That is where you discover your most authentic version of yourself and unlock the infinite possibilities for your life.
- To navigate, you need a different kind of map, not one that tells you where you have been but one yet to be drawn—a Map of the soul.
- If you try to travel forward consulting only the familiar Map of what you have experienced, you will stay stuck in old patterns and wonder why you feel unfulfilled and frustrated. What you create for yourself won't feel right, because you aren't yet the person you need to evolve into.

- If you do what you did, you'll get what you got, so if you want something different, you have to think, choose, and act differently. That requires stepping into the unknown.
- At times in your life, circumstances or your own choices will send you inward on a spiraling journey of self-discovery and self-evolution. This journey to the uncharted can feel disorienting, but you have a navigation tool—intuition—which is your first sense.
- Intuition is your direct line of communication with Spirit, who is always present with you, even when you are unaware of this. When you ask Spirit for help, intuition allows you to understand Spirit's response. Intuition is a tool for dialogue.
- The Realm of Spirit is your true home, where you will find sanctuary and be reminded that Spirit supports you. You "go home" by consciously choosing to feel gratitude.
- Your small self—your ego—identifies with being human and is driven by fear because it has spiritual amnesia: It doesn't remember your true nature as an eternal soul. It doesn't remember that the universe is abundant and that there is always enough.
- When you overcome this "spiritual amnesia," you can still develop spiritual narcolepsy and forget once again that you are a spiritual being, here to play and co-create the world you experience, playing your unique note in the symphony of life!
- In the Realm of Spirit, you can use intuition to consult your soul's Map. There, you can see the pattern created by your soul in its quest to have experiences, and you can decide what actions to take to fulfill your soul's longings.

2

AT HOME IN THE REALM OF SPIRIT

Here's what your soul knows and you forgot: You signed up for this human experience knowing that in this life, you would spend much of your time asleep. In fact, all of us made this choice for ourselves. We agreed we would develop spiritual amnesia and forget that Spirit is the Quintessential Absolute and that we are always a part of Spirit and co-creating with Spirit. We agreed we would get hurt, find happiness, fail, succeed, live, and die. You and I signed up for the whole enchilada. We journeyed away from home, from the Realm of Spirit, to come here. We can't truly go home again until we shed our bodies, but using our consciousness, we can return to this safe spot and remember everything will be okay—life is just a game, and we agreed to play it.

Here's what else we forgot: Spirit is the connective energy in all things great and small, and nothing is ever separate, nothing really dies, everything is recycled and in the process of evolving. Whether or not you believe this with your conscious mind, you can experience this to be true when you return your awareness to your spiritual nature and your connection to the Divine. Reality is much more than what it appears to be.

In fact, before we go any further, I want you to go "home" to the Realm of Spirit and experience your sense of safety and creative flow, using the Awakening the Observing Self exercise that follows this section. When you experience home as a landscape, you also awaken your ability to observe it objectively. Within you awakens the Observer, who will be very helpful when you find yourself feeling unclear and unsteady and yet wanting to remain present in an experience and explore what you can learn from it. The Observer isn't an entity; it's your authentic self.

Your small self (what some call your ego or persona) identifies with emotions and can create all kinds of stories based on those emotional experiences. It assigns meaning to experience that then gets stored in the subconscious as a memory. The small self is the source of judgment and definition—"I feel angry, embarrassed, and sad, because . . . hmm . . . why did I do that? Oh, because I was betrayed. I know what this experience is! Betrayal. Yes. That's very bad. No wonder I feel this way. I'm someone who has been betrayed. I guess I'm the kind of person who gets taken advantage of and betrayed by people I trust. Horrible! File that under Stories of Being Wounded so that I recognize the signs that it's happening again and protect myself. Yep, I'll be very cautious about trusting others now that I understand betrayal."

Your small self thinks it is a brilliant executive, figuring it all out and preparing for the familiar old patterns to show up again. The problem is it doesn't realize it's the one manifesting those patterns! It overidentifies with emotions and memories, and that keeps you stuck in the old stories about who you are and what you can accomplish and experience.

The Observing Self, also known as the soul self, makes no judgments; it's the source of detachment and curiosity. (Think of "Observing Self" as just one of your soul self's nicknames that captures just one of its many abilities.) The Observing Self says, "Hmm, that's interesting. I feel angry, embarrassed, and sad. What's that all about? Ooh, that's interesting! Let's explore it!"

When the Observing Self is active, your experience radically shifts from narrow to vast, from seeing only one facet in a diamond to seeing all sides simultaneously. The soul self knows you exist within a unified greater consciousness called the Great Mind (more on that later), whereas the small self can't fathom this concept. The soul self knows your feelings may have a different meaning from the one your small self wants to automatically assign them.

When the small self is dominating your consciousness, doing its judging and sorting and justifying, the Observing Self is pushed to the background or disabled altogether. But when the Observing Self is awake, there is an immediate integration of both selves. That's what you should be aiming for! Maybe what you're experiencing is what you think it is, but maybe not. Your Observing Self opens your awareness to other possibilities.

The Awakening the Observing Self exercise uses my Total Mindshift Process to help you step back from your emotional reality, observe it as a landscape, and identify its features. Awakening your observing abilities allows you to not feel so immersed in the experience that you identify with it and can't see any way out of it. Since the mind is more powerful than your physical environment, even if you are sitting on a sunny park bench, your mind could be in a treacherous, stormy inner landscape colored by fear and suspicion. And you might be in the exact same physical space as someone else, but if she just won the lottery and you just lost your dog, your internal worlds would determine your experience within your material environment. You would be in different "places," figuratively speaking.

So let's go to the Realm of Spirit and wake up that Observing Self. Just as with any of the exercises in this book, find a quiet, private place to do this exercise, and have your journal or pen and paper handy.

Exercise: Awakening the Observing Self

Sit comfortably and close your eyes.

Tune in to your current state of mind. Without any judgment of yourself—without trying to figure out what you should be feeling or thinking—just describe your state of mind in three adjectives (for example, *happy, mellow, tired* or *angry, fearful, blaming*).

Now, ask yourself, "Where am I?"

Let a landscape comes up in your mind's eye and simply observe it. You might see a meadow filled with poppies and chirping birds—or, conversely, a volcano beside a burned-down forest.

Then open your eyes and write down a description of the place you saw or sensed. You might have seen it vividly, or if you're less visual, you might have gotten an instant knowing that the place would have certain characteristics. Let your imagination wander and deliver you images or information that you just somehow "know." Don't try to force anything. This process requires your unconscious to be actively engaged in showing you symbols and images, and when you relax, it will.

Close your eyes again and allow the place to come up again in your awareness. Now that you're looking at the place rather than being focused on your feelings, pay attention to how your attention is shifting. Notice what is changing.

Then ask yourself, "Who is the one looking at this place?"

Tune your attention to the one who is looking: your Observing Self.

How does this self feel different from the self that sat down at the beginning of this exercise? What words or images come to mind to describe the difference?

Open your eyes and write about what you just observed.

The small self can be thought of as the younger self, brash and a bit of a know-it-all, while the Observing Self is the older and wiser Witness, more philosophical and detached and less reactive to outer circumstances. Remember, the Observing Self is your soul self, which is immortal and directly connected to Source or Spirit.

This Observing Self makes no judgments; it enables you to be discerning, seeing the qualities of something without creating emotions or a story about it. The small self assigns meaning according to memory, which is always colored by our emotional perception. The soul self just observes "cat bite," and doesn't care if cat bites or doesn't bite. It wants to have a full experience. It observes, and it experiences all aspects of the human condition. By working through us, it makes possible the art we make of our human life.

I teach everyone I train in the Total Mindshift Process my favorite thing to say when accessing the Observing Self: "That's interesting."

Now that you have experienced the Observing Self, you can awaken it again to bring yourself home to the Realm of Spirit, a sanctuary you can visit at any time, using the following exercise that picks up where the previous exercise left off.

Exercise: At Home in the Realm of Spirit

When you feel at home in your skin, safe and secure, you are in the Realm of Spirit. Pick a time when you are feeling relaxed; then sit comfortably, close your eyes, and focus on your breathing until you feel even more relaxed. Choose to create a feeling of security and safety within yourself. Then ask yourself, "Where am I?"

What image or idea of a landscape comes into your mind? Pay attention to the qualities of the place you see. What is it—a temple? An open field? A beach? Is there a breeze? What does it feel like against your skin? Is there greenery: grass, bushes, trees, flowers? What is the quality of the light?

Bring your attention now to being in the position of Observing Self. You should immediately begin to sense a calm, mindful detachment as you witness the place from a distance—pull back from it, like a camera backing away from the scene. As you pull away from identifying with the place and the feelings you are experiencing in this landscape, imagine that you see this place is sitting in the hands of Spirit, whose giant hands are made up of sparkling light energy and unconditional love. Pause there for a moment, enjoying the beauty and the grace.

Now allow yourself to move back into the landscape and relax into this unique sanctuary. Wander around the landscape exploring, taking in all that you see and hear. When you are ready, come back into your ordinary consciousness.

Afterward, write down your experiences while exploring this place.

Did you see anyone there?

Were there any animals or objects that stood out for you?

What was it like knowing you were always in the hand of God?

Write about your feelings, or draw a picture to show what you experienced.

TUNING IN TO THE GREATER CONSCIOUSNESS

In the Realm of Spirit, your intuition allows you to attain far greater wisdom than you can in the Realm of Form, the everyday world of the senses, where you're relying on just your five senses and your conscious mind and its intellect to figure out how to change what you don't like about your life. I am in the Realm of Spirit when I am communicating with Fred. I'm not in ordinary, everyday consciousness. I'm in a state of mind that makes me more receptive to communication from Spirit. In this state, I receive communication from spirits too—and lately, as I said, from Fred.

I recognize that the insights of these spirits on the other side of the veil are unfathomably deeper than human knowledge or understanding. They've come to know so much more than we can in this life. I also recognize that they want us to lighten up and stop obsessing about our struggles on earth. In fact, they are so light and loving that they have a great sense of humor. Every time I call the Chorus that speaks to me Fred (and realize I am telling other people about this strange and amazing phenomenon), I remember that. Then, any anxious knots inside me begin to untangle. I know that Fred is always present, and if I stop running around and talking more than listening, I will hear Fred say, "We're here. You forgot who you are and how you began! Do you remember now?" I do, and I remain quiet so I can hear more. I even ask questions, knowing they have answers I can't figure out on my own. They are wise, and they are of Spirit, who is using Fred to communicate with me.

I asked the Chorus known as Fred, "What can we discover when we sail across those uncharted oceans of possibility when there doesn't seem to be a map?"

Fred said, "We are the wet part of the ocean," and "We are We; You are We. We are When You Listen."

When you're in the ocean, it's all wet. Everything is part of the ocean—meaning existence. You don't distinguish between this drop and that one, or this current or that wave. What the Chorus is saying is that we are all one, that they are always there, but we do have to listen to hear them and to bring their voices into this world, into consciousness. It's very challenging to do that when this world and its illusion of separateness feel so very real.

"We are everywhere," says Fred. "We are *all* stories. We are before the beginning and after the end. We are in the experience and in all the parts."

Now, I want to bring something up here before you roll your eyes and stop reading, the way I used to do any time anyone claimed to be receiving channeled information. I'm all about experience, and sharing that experience when something comes of it that can be useful and beneficial to more than just me. And when an experience that feels important to me happens more than once and with consistency, I pay close attention.

In one of my favorite movies, *Oh, God!*, actor George Burns plays the part of God. In one scene he tells the John Denver character that his appearance in the form of an old jokester with a cigar was a choice, explaining that it was the form that John could accept. I wonder if my experience of the Chorus named Fred is in the exact form I can digest. It's true I'm intrigued and interested in what will come of this, given my former prejudice against channeling entities (and my apologies to anyone and everyone in the universe I've ever scoffed at). Fred, Garth (who's the innocent defender of the garden), the manner in which I was opened to listen, the humor, the love and joy I connect with—it all makes me want to go back and listen some more! You may or may not have had this kind of intimate mystical encounter, but I do know how to show you the way to connect. The form will choose itself according to what you need in order to understand Spirit's desire to have you feel your connection and know your true nature.

I decided to ask the Chorus to help me explain this. I immediately fell into the "sugar crash" feeling again (although I'm really hoping that at some point I can be left alert and not head-lolling-slightly-slobbery-half-asleep when Fred communicates to me). This time, I saw a small me with a circle around me, and the word *me* inside a drawing of a radio, and then all kinds of swirling lights around the circle. Then, I heard the Chorus, sounding like a radio announcer, declare, "Radio Fred is everywhere!" and saw a copy of one of my books. I had jokingly referred to a "Quantum Fred" in previous works. Of course! The illusion of the separate self, the ego mind, must see the messenger or guide as "somewhere" outside of the self.

We have to work with what we have: Our capacity to experience, hear, and know a higher form of consciousness is dependent on our willingness to receive, allow, and discern without fear getting in the way. The fear comes from the small self that is determined to be the primary source of information. To know unified consciousness, we must allow the separation to dissolve. In truth, there is no Chorus, no Fred, no me, no you. We are all one. We are all Love.

In *Conversations with God,* writer Neale Donald Walsch has conversations with God through his computer screen. *A Course in Miracles* was channeled through medical psychologist Helen Schucman via a kind of mental dictation from a voice saying it was Jesus. Jane Roberts famously channeled the Seth material, while Esther Hicks still channels the group Abraham. Catholic saint Joan of Arc was visited by Archangel Michael; the visions of St. Hildegard of Bingen are still relevant today. Some people are guided by angels, others by animal spirit guides or other forms of personal guides such as nature devas. The information is what matters, not the form the message or messenger takes.

Fred is my messenger from Spirit, but you will have your own language and personal beliefs about Spirit and wisdom from beyond your own mind's conscious abilities. It doesn't matter whether you've tuned in with direct communication, through a sign in nature, or via a chorus of voices when you meditate. The Divine Consciousness, known by many names and taking many forms, has infinite ways to get your attention and get across the message that you are not alone—not ever.

I take comfort in knowing that I'm never alone, even if it feels that way sometimes because like everyone, I can sometimes slip into spiritual amnesia. Actually feeling the interconnectedness helps, because the world of the senses, what I call the Realm of Form, feels so real that it starts to feel like the only reality, and you can start to think you aren't really connected to Spirit, that your mind made up that belief. The small self is utterly convinced it's out there alone, on its own. The small self forgets about the presence of Spirit, and the presence of your larger self that encompasses the small self. It is this larger self, the soul self, that is the true you in all your glory, and your soul is very different. The best way to describe it is as an impersonal self, an observer that stewards your experience on earth. It is wise and powerful and doesn't identify with the same things that the small self gets caught up in. It's there to help the small self evolve so that the whole of humanity evolves. It's the active link to Divine Will but needs the small self to cooperate in the co-creative and evolutionary process.

The small self thinks it has to find its way without a compass or any sort of guide other than a very limited Map of what you and others have experienced. That is not the Map that will show you the way to a deep sense of purpose and meaning. It is not the Map that is going to help you satisfy the yearnings of your soul. What you need is your soul's Map, which guides you to experience magic in the uncharted places.

YOUR OWN RELATIONSHIP WITH SPIRIT

Working within the limitations of the small self, all human beings seem destined to be more concerned with the form of something than the energy it creates. We tend to have distinct ideas about the form that abundance or love should arrive in. No wonder when it shows up right in front of our eyes, we can completely overlook it! But when you orient yourself in the Realm of Spirit and access the Map of the soul, you recognize that you do have what you most desire. You're never without abundance or love—but you certainly can be lacking the *forms* of abundance and love that your small self seeks. The small self wants it "just so," while the soul is open to the beautiful, unexpected magic of Spirit. It understands that some pain is inevitable, but pain doesn't have to define your life or be amplified by a fear-driven trek through the familiar places. Guess what? There be dragons there too. But the magic in the familiar will escape you if you remain stuck in the mind-set of the small self. Where's the magic? Outside the lines drawn by your small self, outside the conformity you think is safe and certain, outside the man-made constructs for the world and your place in it.

So don't be afraid, even though I can't promise you the kind of magic that erases all possibility of suffering. I know sometimes you get discouraged. When you don't have financial security, when the check doesn't clear and you lose the job, when the one you love deeply cheats on you or walks away, when your dog dies—of *course* you'll be in pain. And your small self wants to protect you from that. Your soul, however, has a broader perspective. It knows that in the uncharted waters of not being able to pay your bills for the first time in your life, of not knowing when you'll get a job and feel safe again, there is a lesson to be learned and a discovery to be made. It knows when your marriage is eroding and you've lost sight of solid ground, as it knows when you've achieved everything you think you wanted but still feel there must be more or something else to fill your purpose. Your soul knows that you are right where you need to be to have the experiences you need. Trust it.

We think of life as a linear journey, so we make a goal of reaching a particular destination. Then we see everything we experience as a separate part of a chronological, sequential story, one we hope makes us happy, one in which we hope we can find love and safety and meaning. But when the plotline of the story upsets us and makes us feel scared, angry, or sad, we run for shelter and safety. We listen to the small self, which is the source of our fear. The small self says, "Safety? That's my department! I'll keep you safe! Follow me!" Then the soul says, "Ah, she's not listening. Okay, I'll hang back and let the ego take the wheel and navigate for a while. When she is ready, I'll nudge her and make her aware of me again."

Spirit is always connected to your soul and wants to help you because it is within you as well as everywhere else. Spirit is not a consciousness that is external—a deity that is somewhere up in the sky. We are made of the substance of Spirit, and through your soul self, the tiny spark of Spirit individuated as you, Spirit wants you to know that true safety lies in experiencing this inherent connection to Divine Intelligence. This is the lifeline always available for you to communicate through, like a walkie-talkie or cell phone that is always charged.

Too often, we don't answer the call from Spirit to dialogue with this loving Creator and Great Mind. In fact, we forget there's a phone. Ring-a-ding ding? We forget how to connect and how good it feels when we're communicating with Spirit. (Later, you'll learn more about how to dialogue with Spirit.)

Decades ago, I had lost all the magic of knowing my spiritual connection. I'd become totally cut off from communication with Spirit. I hid from my feelings and tried to dull my pain by drinking, using drugs, and seeking temporary pleasures to escape the turmoil inside me. I survived violence, low self-worth, and all the behaviors that accompanied my story of being a victim. And when I couldn't take it anymore, I was able to hit bottom. Thank God! Then through grace and a spiritual awakening I became sober. It was as if I'd been struck by lightning. I have been sober and on a spiritual path ever since. My life wasn't working for me—addiction tore my world apart and affected everyone in it and I was miserable—until I surrendered to Spirit. I oriented myself in Spirit's realm, and then my own soul's Map became visible to me. What a gift!

I have maintained my sobriety, worked as a metaphysical intuitive counselor, and been a medium for more than a quarter century. Spiritual practices are a part of my life every day. Even so, I'm not immune to recurrences of spiritual amnesia. I've resisted following my soul's Map at times because like everyone, I like to avoid uncertainty and discomfort. *Where's the easy road? Yeah, I'll take that one!* I hear the voice of my small self as it loudly whines, "Wah

wah wah, listen to me! The sky is falling, run, fight, force, seize the controls, hide!" But by following the Map of my soul, I've come to understand how I can help you follow yours. Miracles can and do happen without much effort when you know how to wake up and what Map to use.

THE ILLUSION OF CERTAINTY

Eighty percent of my clients have come to me precisely to see what their future portends (because as an intuitive counselor, I can access information about what is likely to happen in their future). People want certainty that the story they want to tell will come to fruition. I've always been able to see the potentials of a person's life from the vantage point I'm provided, but in the end, it's impossible to know everything that is going to happen to us. And we can't have complete control over what happens. But we can feel better knowing that infinite possibilities and our greatest potential have yet to be discovered in the uncharted. Only the soul can discover them and gift them to the small self for integration. The soul comes to earth knowing it wants certain experiences, but it's open to what unfolds. It is up for the adventure. And that adventure happens within the power of a 24-hour day. We co-create our future now, not tomorrow or sometime down the road. The soul knows that infinite potential is ignited in the now. All the power we ever need is revealed as an experience in each present moment to present moment.

In my work, I often chat with the people who have fallen off the edge of their life's Map and suffered tremendous upheaval and disaster, yet they're fine—because they are feeling their connection to Spirit. We're never truly prepared for the tragedies that can befall us, but I know intimately that there is something beyond our imaginations waiting for us to experience it. And *it's all good.* That is precisely what Fred wants us to discover before we get over "there." This is the transformation Spirit wants us to experience now, so we can know our true power and responsibility to the world we reside in when we're still embodied here in the material world. We just need to lighten up and enjoy the adventure so we can continue doing what we came here to do. Believe me, this kind of intimate knowing is more valuable than certainty about the future—and better yet, this knowing is attainable. Certainty, not so much.

We all seek the comfort of certainty—a "place" or state of mind that we can call home. If you've ever been at sea for a long time without glimpsing land, you know it can be unsettling and isolating. You can even start to feel a little scared about when you will see land again. You know it's there, but where is it? Human beings, like other animals, need some territory with a boundary that they can know is their own, a sanctuary to retreat to that provides a break from the challenges of our journey.

When my family sailed across the Atlantic on a vacation in the early 1970s, a much different and more nausea-producing experience than the trips people take on the beautifully balanced cruise ships of today, I remember my father telling us not to be alarmed if we began to feel disoriented—and to keep our eyes on the horizon. There would always be a horizon even if there was no land for days. The horizon is the fixed spot, where changes don't make your stomach churn and your heart start to race in anxiety. By looking at a "something," my father told my sister and me, we could orient ourselves in our surroundings, which seemed to go on forever beyond what the eye could see.

And so it's only natural that when we look out across those uncharted waters of our life's new adventure without a fixed spot to gaze on, we may become disoriented and unsure of ourselves, not knowing who we'll become when we reach wherever it is we're supposed to be going or that there will be a "there" to reach at all. The protection familiarity offers, the promise of home in this material world, the Realm of Form, is an illusion. Everything changes, and that's how life is meant to be. Clinging to the old ways of doing things because you're afraid is just going to lead to suffering. You might as well admit you have to engage in this uncertain adventure called life. You have to be brave and enter the uncharted places so you can discover who you really are and how much power and light you have within you.

It is time for a new human and a new earth to evolve into being, and you are a part of that. It's exciting but scary, too. Fortunately, you are not alone—and you have a Map.

THE MAP THAT WILL HELP YOU FIND "HOME"

The Map of the small self is two-dimensional and flat and features familiar places—it tells you where you have been. When your best laid plans go astray, and you don't know what to do next, you realize this Map isn't as helpful as you'd thought. You might start distrusting this Map of yours and thinking you're a victim of bad luck or the old man god has forsaken you or maybe he never even existed. You might figure there are no Maps, really, and we're all just muddling through aimlessly, lost and unable to get "home" to a sense of safety and purpose. Ultimately, the more faith you put in the Map of your small self, the more your capacity to see the truth of your surroundings will become distorted.

The familiar Map that has served you well just isn't the right tool for the job when you are faced with the uncertainty that comes with the journey into the uncharted. If you rely on the familiar Map with its features etched upon it by your experiences and memories, your perceptions and perspective will be based on the limitations of the *small self.*

And you will have terrible trouble finding home.

Home is not a physical place but a state of being. It's like the kingdom of God, which the Bible says is at hand. "At hand" means right there, invisible but *there,* in the Realm of Energy into which all of creation, including ourselves, is integrated. "Home" is the state of consciousness in which you feel gratitude and safety because you're experiencing your soul and your connection to Spirit. Home is the Realm of Spirit.

You can get back home to the Realm of Spirit and rest there at any time. I've shown you an exercise you can use to do this, and there are other ways to access this realm as well: prayer, meditation, letting yourself feel gratitude for the gift of your life and Spirit's constant presence. My way home is by closing my eyes and saying, "Thank you."

If you have spiritual amnesia, which happens when you don't "check in" with Spirit very often using spiritual practices, home is hard to find. You start wandering in circles and getting nowhere, repeating the same old mistakes. You keep entering the mall through the wrong entrance, orienting yourself from the wrong vantage point—that is, by holding the Map of your small self and saying, "What is the problem here? I'm *trying* to avoid troubles, and I just keep ending up back in the same old place. What is up with this lousy Map? Am I crazy? I know I'm not stupid or blind. What the heck is happening?"

Wrong Map.

When you view the world through the limits of your *small self,* you see only the separated parts of the material world. You are guided by your personal narratives that tell you who you are based on your past experience, ambitions, and goals that were set within the Realm of Form. You're oblivious to being part of one big matrix of interconnectedness. You forget where home is, and you feel lost.

The *soul self* knows that regardless of how things look when you're scared, or totally in your head, or focused on achievement, you have a soul Map that is magical and multidimensional. It knows that to unlock the secrets of this Map, you need to take your eyes away from the Realm of Form and allow the world to show you its magic. Your small self needs to come into alignment with your soul self instead of trying to run the show all on its own, and this happens automatically when you orient yourself in the Realm of Spirit. The small self will shut up and listen! The conflict between the yearnings of your soul and the desires of your small self will get resolved.

So what does this alignment of soul self and small self look like in the world of the senses? A friend of mine had to attend a legal deposition. If you've never been deposed, it can be intimidating, because you're facing questioners who want to trip you up and cause you to make mistakes that can hurt you or others. She asked for my advice, and I told her to orient herself in the Realm of Spirit and focus on the highest good for all concerned. I intuited that her soul and the souls of the people involved in the case had chosen to have this experience. Her job was to remain oriented in the Realm of Spirit—ahh! Safety! Home! Love!—and speak the truth, simply and without embellishment and explanations, for the good of everyone.

Afterward, she told me she was very surprised at how calm she had been. She had not become upset or scared even when she was mentally fatigued. She was able to speak her simple truth and defend her own actions and choices without feeling on the defensive. She remained confident despite the fact that she realized she had made some mistakes in the past that the lawyers grilled her about. Even getting the papers mixed up while testifying didn't make her flustered. Because my friend was working with her soul's Map, she knew exactly what words to say. She knew she could pause and collect her thoughts. She didn't have to try to figure out how she might outsmart the lawyers to ensure she would feel safe. She just felt safe—*even though she was vigilant about not making any mistakes.*

That's how you want to go through life: present and aware moment to moment, facing challenges without going into panic mode, alert without being guided by fear. Confidence allows you to sail into the uncharted places, and meet up with those dragons without having to get burned. Tread cautiously, by all means. That dragon breath is fierce! But don't freak out and let your small self take over when a dragon shows up. You can actually train that dragon to be your ally and serve you, as you'll learn later, so don't be afraid!

I'll help you deal with the nitty-gritty of facing your fears and reclaiming your personal power when we get to Chapter 5. But first I want you to get a perspective on the twisting, turning roads your soul sometimes takes you on so you can start developing more trust in your soul's Map, the one that takes you to uncharted places where magic awaits you.

Traveler's Notes

- All of us agreed before incarnating into human form that in this lifetime, we would spend much of our time asleep to our spiritual nature. We agreed that our job would be to remember who we are and to remain awake as much as we can.
- Life is an adventure and a game—one that you agreed to play. Fred, the Chorus of spirits, says we have to lighten up and remember to be joyful.
- The small self has two purposes: to try to keep us safe from harm and hurt and to help us express ourselves in the Realm of Form, in our lives on earth, in a unique way.
- The soul is aware of the small self, but the small self is usually not aware of the soul. Whenever the Observing Self—your ability to see what you are experiencing as you experience it and not feel anger or fear—dominates your consciousness, your small self remembers that there is a soul it is integrated into. Then the soul self can aid you in co-creation.
- To awaken your soul, which serves as the Observing Self, bring yourself home to the Realm of Spirit. Then this wise, powerful, impersonal self will guide you and help your small self evolve.
- Everything is always changing. The real safety and security lie not in knowing the future, but in knowing your true nature and knowing that your home is in the Realm of Spirit.
- Home is not a physical place but a state of being in which you experience and are aware of your soul and your connection to Spirit. If you have spiritual amnesia, which happens when you don't "check in" with Spirit using spiritual practices, home is hard to find.

- When you have spiritual amnesia, you start wandering in circles, feeling lost, caught in old patterns and not seeing your role in co-creating what you are experiencing. You feel disconnected from Spirit and forget that you have a home.
- Your small self needs to align with your soul self instead of trying to run the show all on its own.
- As soon as you orient yourself in the Realm of Spirit, you still see the dangers that the small self was frightened by, but you feel safe.

3

WHEN YOU END UP ON THE SCENIC ROUTE

Some of you know I love to ride my Harley. For me, riding a motorcycle is a personal symbol of spiritual fitness and living free and a way to stay fully present in the moment. My husband, Marc, and I take the back roads—the scenic routes—and enjoy the view and the ride. Sometimes we stick with the more familiar and boring route because it's faster and we have a lot we want to do, but we recognize that even if you are feeling pressed for time and you take a "wrong" turn onto the "wrong" road, it's all good. You're just on the "scenic route." There's always something to discover, always something of beauty. The best thing to do when you find yourself here is take a deep breath, keep your eyes open, and stay in the present instead of worrying about what might happen in the future if you don't get back on track right away. Your intuition will guide you to what to do next.

Riding a motorcycle requires you to be completely in a zone of present time awareness. Motorcycling is a dangerous sport, and you need to be calmly alert and aware of everything around you at all times. It's an amazing feeling to be so present minded.

When you take an unexpected detour and find yourself on the scenic route in your own life, you can get frustrated and give yourself a face-palm, or you can stay fully present while you tune in to what this road has to offer and what your options are. Sometimes the unexpected journey turns out to be even more delightful than the original route would have been. Taking the scenic route isn't always efficient—but where do you want to go, anyway? Seriously, maybe you were on the wrong road!

Many of us get stuck thinking we have to do this or that in order to be happy. Remember, your soul yearns for experience. Maybe that can't be found if you are rushing through life, taking the roads clearly marked on the Map that is familiar to you. What if you were to make choices from the truest part of you and choose a path that takes you to uncharted places? What would your life be like then? Would the back roads be unwanted and uncomfortable detours, or would they be magical, uncharted places of discovery?

When you find the courage to listen to your intuition, step off the familiar path, and explore the unknown, you will be following the calling of your soul. That's what you are here for. You will get to where you were supposed to go—which you decided upon long before you came into this life. Your destination is not a place but an experience, and there are many ways to have that experience.

In my work, I've often talked about detours, when you forget what you were called to do and end up doing something entirely different. The fact is that all roads lead to Rome. Eventually, regardless of what you choose to do, you will end up having the experiences you came here for. You may have spiritual amnesia and find yourself getting lost again and again, but your soul is always right there next to you, waiting for you to wake up and pay attention to what it has to tell you. It will make sure you have the experiences it wants you to have, even when you're taking every back road and "wrong" turn. Trust it!

When you add your light to the sum of Light and co-create wholeheartedly, mindfully, and respectfully in community with others, you are doing what you came here to do. You will be on the right road even if it seems you are taking the long way and wasting time. If you think about it, why wouldn't you take the scenic route rather than the highway? Are you in a rush to get somewhere?

What's the destination? Get rid of the mentality that you are going "to" some specific place on the Map—trying to create some specific situation that will allow you to be happy ever after. Life will always change, and you will always be in motion.

So the scenic route is a back road—not the most direct, fastest way to what you think you want to experience. Guess what? You can experience joy, abundance—whatever you seek—wherever you are. And your soul may want something more: the experience of opening your heart and your eyes in compassion. You may have to take a back road to have that experience because you probably don't have "develop deeper understanding of people who frustrate me" and "experience the bittersweetness of life" on your small self's list of goals to accomplish. Remember, your soul takes winding paths to get the experiences it wants to have. It is working with Spirit to co-create a reality your small self might not be conscious of—although you *can* become more conscious of how you got onto a back road if you do the work in this book!

I often talk about co-creating with Spirit the reality you want to experience, and let me just say something about the root word: *create*. You *are* creative, even if you aren't a singer, writer, dancer, or painter. All of us are. Creativity isn't just about the fine arts. It's the life force itself. Nature is always creating, giving birth to something new—and that means old things die away. Even so, nothing's ever wasted. It's all recycled and born again into some new form.

The pain you experienced is not wasted either. It can break open your heart wider than you thought possible and help you to heal yourself and others. It can make you wise and compassionate—and help you find your purpose and destiny. When Fred says, "It's all good," it doesn't mean the terrible things that have happened to you are a blessing. It does mean that blessings can come out of them. There's a Garth Brooks song called "Unanswered Prayers" whose lyrics beautifully capture the reality that we can want something desperately and pray, "Please, oh please, oh please," *not* get our prayers answered, and someday be deeply grateful that Spirit said no. Spirit has three answers to prayers: *Yes*; *Not right now;* and *No, because I have something better in mind that is in sync with the desires of your soul.* Spirit's ideas about what to co-create with you are much more brilliant than you can imagine.

Here's how it works between you and Spirit. You, as an individual, are always *co*-creating. The divine creative force is always there with you, along with spirits and allies who enthusiastically join in as you co-create reality. And you are never alone. We are all storytellers, and if we listen deeply and share honestly, we will find that wonderful feeling of community and wisdom in the archetypal themes we all share as we evolve collectively—themes such as freedom, playfulness, mastery, and learning. None of us is meant to be an island, isolating and hoarding resources. When we share our wisdom and support and resources with others, we immediately dispel the illusion of scarcity. We remember that the matrix of connection sustains us regardless of what we want to create or what form our creativity takes.

If you are willing to step into those uncharted waters, leaving your old self behind with love to discover who you really are and why you're here, you will find that you'll be in a collaborative process. You always have access to the guidance of Spirit, and you always have your soul's Map.

DON'T PANIC ABOUT THE TIME

When did you get off track and onto a back road? How did you end up dissatisfied and wanting your life to change—or facing changes you don't want instead of attracting the situations you do want?

I know it's hard to be patient when your life isn't going as you want it to. But if you remain in your small self, walking only on the familiar path and using only your rational mind, planning and strategizing and figuring everything out and then taking action, quick, before opportunities dry up, you will probably end up lost and upset. Don't rush to get back on what you think is the interstate!

The small self is very much aware of time ticking away. But Fred, free from the limitations of time and space, has a message: "All in due time. Things happen as they are meant to happen." When I asked

Fred about the meaning of time, I was hoping to get a brilliant flash of insight, some deeper understanding I could impart—maybe something like the Mayan calendar with its multitude of layers depicting the different dimensions of time and experience. I thought perhaps Fred would have a brilliant discourse with me on the evolution of the noosphere that I teach about in my certification programs. But instead they embraced me with their humming energy and happiness and echoed my own words back to me, sounding eerily like what I had said to a coaching client earlier that afternoon: "Take your focus off of temporary outer conditions. They were set in motion by the past. Go empty. Leave time; leave space. Remember we are abundance! Smile! Smile! Smile! Wake up! It's Party Time!"

I came to clearly knowing I did not, nor would I *ever*, say "Party Time." But I get it. We need to recognize that what we see now is a product of our thinking, beliefs, choices, and actions, set in motion by something in the past and now present in form in front of us. In response, we should practice curiosity and feel grateful for the presence of Spirit and the potential for miracles. Slow down, and you will quiet the anxiety of your small self, which is freaking out about the passage of time. Opportunities come around again, and what you experience along the way on the scenic route may be crucial to your life journey. Have you ever seen that play out in your life?

You don't always know where life will take you when you are guided by your soul's Map, but that's also true if you rely solely on your familiar Map! Our journeys are meant to be complex. When you follow the soul's Map instead of the familiar one, every step is magical and infused with meaning. When you recognize Spirit as the intelligent force of the matrix that holds everything together, the whole Map lights up. You step back in awe of how synchronicities prove this inherent connection, and you see evidence of your co-creative collaboration with Spirit. You feel a sense of safety because now you can see it's all good—even detouring onto a back road.

But then, you'll suddenly nod off again due to spiritual narcolepsy. This typically happens when you have been triggered by something that reminds you of a past experience and fear sucks you back into the illusion of separation from your soul and Spirit. Don't panic! Orient yourself in the Realm of Spirit. And realize you may have to pull off the road and stop your life to do it.

WHEN I TOOK AN IMPORTANT DETOUR

Stopping to self-reflect is crucial because if you avoid it, your soul will find a way to get you to do it. It does this by making sure you experience an illness, an accident, or a loss that is so shocking that you find yourself sitting down and asking, "What is this about?"

It happened to me not long ago. I was not in my lane, literally or figuratively. Literally, I was riding a brand-new Harley my husband had bought me for my birthday. True to form, I wanted to ride the newest and fastest one. It was bigger than my last bike, and as soon as I got her, I knew she didn't fit me. (Yes, we riders refer to our bikes as "she"—and give them names too.) It felt as if I were riding on a wild Arabian horse. I didn't listen to my inner voice that kept saying we were not a fit. After riding this bike for two weeks, I went too fast around a corner on the Seacoast Highway, promptly crashed into six granite posts, and was thrown into someone's field. My beautiful, gleaming white Heritage Softail motorcycle was destroyed, and I was rushed to a hospital.

Figuratively, I was out of my lane because I had just made a big career change and was in denial of my calling and my purpose. For a multitude of reasons, fear and false pride fueled me into changing lanes, and traveling in one that didn't completely suit me but seemed safer. I didn't realize this until I was stuck at home in bed for the summer unable to walk with a mangled right leg and broken left foot, and asking myself that question: "So what is this all about?"

I had gotten off track about a year before. Although I had received a lot of opportunities to be presented to the world as an intuitive and personal development author, I was still deeply struggling with the perception of my work. No matter how many people saw what I did as meaningful and deep, I still had not truly accepted myself—specifically, my intuitive gifts and how they were evolving into mediumship. I had other plans! Ultimately, I would have to find myself and let my soul tell me the truth. If I didn't, nothing in my life was going to work for long. But I didn't know that yet.

The essence of my efforts was that I was trying to rebrand myself as more mainstream. In extreme contrast to where I am today, back then I really fought to try to control how others would see me. I didn't want to be perceived as too much of a "woo-woo" person (who was I kidding?) who spoke to the dead. My career was flourishing, so it seemed I was on the right track. I was thrilled!

I published a new book with a mainstream book publisher that understood my desire to "get away from the woo-woo," and in promoting it, I was booked on a network TV talk show. I discussed my new book and the science behind my own experience of stress and weight. I felt I did a great job and was being taken seriously. I felt safe in this situation, and very much accepted. I also appeared on a very well-known, mainstream talk show to do some intuitive readings. It was a fantastic publicity break, so although it was focused on my intuitive work instead of the topic of my book, I accepted the opportunity.

I was in top form during the tapings, but what should have been a moment of triumph soon turned into a nightmare. After the show aired, Internet trolls began to attack me, even threaten me. Of course, I realize now that as soon as anyone becomes too public they become targets for bullying, but this had never happened to me before with quite such intensity. This time, the comments were full of hatred, and I was attacked categorically—as if I represented the entirety of all psychics and healers who should be burnt at the stake. It brought up a lot of unresolved childhood issues, triggering a fear of persecution and a deep sense of the shame of being different that went back to my early years, and of course my own family history as the daughter of a Holocaust survivor (I'll talk more about that in more detail in Chapter 5). The feeling was compounded when I got a letter beautifully written by a pastor of a Southern church enclosing a petition signed by people praying for me because it appeared I didn't know that I was actually doing the work of the devil. At least they were nice about it, but that pretty much did it. I was so mortified that I vowed not to let anything like this happen again. There were enough psychic mediums in the world. I could find a way to provide my skill in service to something more practical! So I decided (rather, my small self decided) to rebrand myself as an intuitive business coach and strategist, talking about practical ways to apply intuition and teaching and training coaches to use my techniques. I was already successful at this, with a flourishing school and a small group of powerful influencers who found this service helpful. So to stay safe, my small self declared it was time to dial down the woo-woo! I told the branding experts. I was done with that!

But I wasn't.

The truth is that you can create success in the material world by working hard and being smart, which I did! But if you're not authentic within that success, the experience will be unsatisfying. Instead of a sense of "Good, I'm where I belong!" I felt, "Okay, I'm really good at this, and it's a valid and valuable skill, but I'm not feeling totally at home just doing what I'm doing. I'm missing something."

I remember being invited to speak at a conference filled with brilliant business leaders. I felt I should be excited, but when I got there, well, you know that children's song that goes, "One of these things is not like the others"? No matter how fabulous it was being around these people, I felt I did not belong there. I was not in my lane! (Never mind that two or three of the business leaders knew I was an intuitive and took me aside to ask me questions of a metaphysical and spiritual nature rather than anything about business strategy!)

It was obvious that my soul was nudging me to break out of the confines of conformity and explore the uncharted places where the magic was. I had yet to meet Fred! I had no idea that my soul's path had that incredible experience waiting for me. What I do know now is that I was being called out of my world where nothing was working and all my ideas were falling short. My soul knew that I needed to stop letting my fear dictate my route and instead become fully authentic, letting myself express the beautiful gifts I was given to help others. The accident came at the perfect time. I needed to stop what I was doing.

And the trip to the hospital? It helped birth an epiphany and gave me an opportunity to start doing the work of integrating the experience and the insights it gave me. I look back now and think how fortunate that synchronicity brought all the pieces together to make me stay put and contemplate my choices. If I didn't do that, I was going to fall back into spiritual amnesia. I had to remain conscious that I was in uncharted territory and forced into deep reflection on what I wanted to co-create and who I had to become now. This is work—and you can't avoid it.

The self-reflection in my sickbed made me face up to my deep-seated tendency toward people pleasing. I had to face up to it if I was going to remain in this uncharted territory of self-discovery and co-creative evolution instead of running back to familiar territory. I had temporarily forgotten Spirit and had quickly found that this path my small self chose was not my lane at all. I was in the lane determined by my self-centered fear, not by my soul. Now that I'm fully riding in my lane, no longer hiding or trying to control how others see me, I'm really happy that I was forced by circumstances to take out the Map of my soul to consider the exhilarating possibility of traveling to the uncharted places that would lead to my authentic and most fulfilling life.

Have you resisted the call of your soul out of fear of what others might think? Does it feel too hard to stay in your lane? Have you tried to make something work because it looks good on the outside, dimmed your light, and made yourself small in order to be accepted and fit in? I know I'm not alone in doing this. If you are completely honest with yourself, I will wager you identify with my story, even if just a little bit. Our culture sets us up to stay small, listen to our self-centered fears, and just do the same old same old. We're allowed to be different—but not too much—so we only shine within the parameters of what is accepted.

Yes, you feel vulnerable when you step away from the familiar and acceptable, and it takes courage to be yourself. For me, there was no other way. I've come to the realization that I am here to use my unusual gifts and not put them under a bushel out of a sense of shame for being so different or fear that I will be bullied. My light is the light of Spirit, and it needs to shine.

So does yours.

THE COURAGE TO ACKNOWLEDGE YOUR LANE AND STAY IN IT

In Thunder Bay, Ontario, a few months after my accident, still uneasy and uncertain of which direction to take, I was given a real gift and had another epiphany that pointed me back toward my lane. The weather was 47 degrees below zero (Celsius) and I thought no one would come to what I thought would be my last "woo-woo" event. Instead, 400 people filled the audience, and for three hours I gave some of the most profound readings of my career. It was as if my soul said to my small self, "Okay, you sit this one out. Lemme show you how it's done." Then my heart opened up and I finally got it.

I knew I was home. I knew it didn't matter anymore who said what, who bullied on the Internet, or who showed up and who didn't. As long as I was being true to my calling, all would be well. For the first time in my life, I just knew why I was here in this life. It didn't matter how successful I would be or not. What mattered was that I was doing a service I was born to do and in my small way could help people heal and find hope. I called my husband and said, "I know we tried to go in the other direction, but I don't have a right to withhold this ability of mine from others. We need to change course." Not at all surprised and totally relieved that I had stopped running from my gift, my husband hugged me as soon as I got home and life got right-sized. It was a very hard lesson, but now I was home.

So my lane, as it turns out, is the lane where I still do all the things I mentioned. Yes, I serve in many ways, but I also talk to dead people—and sometimes to my guides, known as Fred. Whether people laugh at me or dismiss me or not, this is what I do. It's my lane, and I'm staying in it. And in this lane, I ride free, and that is powerful for me.

We all have a lane, but the stories of our past, which fuel our fear, can keep us from discovering it or compel us to leave it once we have found it. Sometimes we find our lane early but give it up. Our fear of being shamed or ridiculed, or getting hurt in some other way, causes us to tune out our soul's calling. Maybe we compare ourselves with others and think that someone else's lane looks better, so we want to copy that. There—that person must know the secret, so let's be like them! Does that resonate for you? If it does, can you identify why you decided to ignore your soul and instead take a familiar and seemingly safe road?

Let me share with you a reading that really brought home this idea of fear and shame making us hide our light and try to be something or someone we're not. A man I'll call Paul had attended one of my events with his wife, hoping that they would connect to the spirit of a deceased family member. Instead, the last person on earth this man wanted to hear from showed up instead: Paul's father, Jim, who had crossed over and wanted to communicate to him.

For me, the experience of being the go-between was rich with detail, almost a visceral experience. I could even *smell* Jim—an acrid sweat tinged with anger and fear. I saw Jim the way he wanted me to: barrel-chested, with a beer in his hand, being sarcastic and verbally abusive to his son. Jim showed me how he belittled Paul throughout his life and how every time Paul had an idea or aspiration, Jim would call him stupid.

Now Jim wanted Paul to know he'd been wrong, and that he had been abused himself and didn't know how to be a parent. He was sorry that his actions caused Paul to adopt certain beliefs about his life, and now he wanted his son to let that story go. Paul was brilliant, Jim insisted. Jim took responsibility for the fact that he had forced his son to dim his light and consequently choose to be around others who would perpetuate that narrative.

Jim was very clear that Paul's ideas about what he wanted to create were good. He said that Paul needed to follow his dreams and never let anyone take them away again. It was up to Paul now to write a new story for himself.

After I relayed these messages, I saw emotion written all over Paul's face. At last he was receiving the acceptance and validation he had desperately wanted from his father but had never received while his father was alive.

What do you do when everything you have believed about who you are, what you're capable of, how smart or not you are, how lovable you are is challenged by an experience with the spirit of the very person who set those stories in motion?

There was no mistaking that this was truly Jim speaking to Paul, and now Paul was being given an invitation into a new version of himself. Would he have the courage to face uncharted places within him, discard the old beliefs he held, heal the dynamics of his relationships that fostered the old story, and stay in his lane—where his soul wanted to be? Or would he develop spiritual amnesia and end up on the old roads once again, dissatisfied with his life and feeling bad about himself?

Whether it is individual spirits or my Chorus, Fred, their urgent message is the same. It is time for us to *let it go.* We have to discard our old ideas of who we are, ideas that are based on our wounds, and choose instead to express our whole selves. The soul and the small self must align if we're to become the powerful co-creators we're meant to be.

Earlier, I talked about the small self's motive to keep us safe. The small self also has another motive: to help us express ourselves in the Realm of Form, in our lives on earth, in a unique way. When the small self is open to hearing the soul, it serves as the soul's paintbrush. The small self's job is to allow the soul to have experiences in this lifetime, to know what it's like to be male or female, healthy or ill, strong or weak, playful or serious. Our individuality is what determines our own special highway. When the small self is not in a frantic state, trying to protect us from harm, we experience the world through it and it helps us to co-create the reality we seek.

The small self always has some ideas about form and experience that are in sync with the soul—and it has some ideas that are not. Our task is to regularly slow down and become fully present as we observe the scenery around us, whether it's a beautiful corridor of trees whose leaves are turning color or a hospital room. Once we are still and present, we have to listen patiently as we wait for inner wisdom to arise into our awareness. This is important if we're to get back into our lane!

One way to slow down and listen is through journaling. Journaling lets you remain open and present instead of becoming distracted. You can do it before you go to bed at night or when you first wake up, throughout the day when the mood strikes you or at a particular time you designate as a good point for you to stop what you're doing and orient yourself in the world of Spirit. (As I mentioned, throughout this book I'll offer some journaling exercises for you to do and some other exercises that you might want to journal about after you've completed them.)

The following is a journaling exercise you might want to use to help you discover where you have been and where you want to go. Take your time with it because this type of self-reflective work is important to your soul.

Exercise: What's on Your Map?

To do this exercise, take time away from distractions and begin by spending a few minutes simply sitting comfortably with closed eyes, observing your breath as you inhale and exhale. Don't pay attention to any thoughts or images that come into your mind as you focus on your breath—just let them go. When you feel a shift in your energy—a greater sense of calm—open your eyes, take out a journal and pen, and answer the following questions.

Who do I need to become to live the life I desire?

What do I need to let go of in order to become that version of myself so I can live that life?

What are the stories I've believed and accepted about myself based on how I was wounded?

Have I accepted certain things because they're familiar, rather than because it's how I chose them to be? And if so, how have those stories I've believed held me back?

If the person who wounded me were to make amends and set me free from the old story, what would I have to do differently?

What have I gained from the old stories about myself (seeing myself as flawed, unlovable, stupid, unteachable, unworthy, etc.)?

What have I lost from seeing myself as so flawed?

When faced with a new opportunity, how do I behave automatically?

What am I willing to sacrifice to become the person who is worthy enough, smart enough, etc., to achieve my dreams?

What is my "lane"? Why do I believe that is my lane?

When you are finished, sit for a minute or two. Notice any feelings that come up. Write them down, along with any thoughts you have about having answered these questions.

Now write your answer to this question: *Where do I want to go?*

And to this one: *What is my "lane"?*

If you don't know the answers, that's okay. If you have answers but they're vague, that's okay too. You are starting to discover what your soul knows. You now have deeper insights into where you have been, where you want to go, why you want to take this journey, and what you have to discard or take up in order to reach your destination. You are closer to understanding you and the calling of your soul.

Your soul's Map is starting to become more visible.

So what happens when you let go of the old stories and decide to listen to your soul as it takes you on a scenic route? You have experiences that your soul always wanted you to have. And you take a journey—not to a destination in the Realm of Form, but to the uncharted. Because there, as your soul well knows, is where you have the potential to make the most of this life and evolve into who you came here to be—the best possible you.

Traveler's Notes

- When you take a "wrong turn" and end up in a situation you didn't plan for, don't worry. You are just on the scenic route in your soul's adventure.
- When you find yourself on the scenic route, go home to the Realm of Spirit and remain fully present in the situation to see what you can discover. Let intuition be your guide.
- Rushing through life, taking only familiar roads, denies your soul the experiences it seeks. Your soul may intervene so that it can get to its destination—not a place but an experience.
- Your soul yearns to co-create wholeheartedly, mindfully, and respectfully, in community with others.
- By nature, you are creative, even if you are not an artist, because creativity is the essence of the life force itself.
- Tragedies and traumas are not blessings, but blessings can come out of them.
- Scarcity is dispelled when we connect with others and share wisdom and support. Then we remember we are interconnected with Spirit, the source of endless abundance.
- The small self worries about temporary conditions, not realizing they were set in motion by conditions of the past and are already beginning to change.
- The small self is impatient and scared and wants certainty right away. It has trouble accepting that things happen as they are meant to happen.
- Slow down, be curious, and feel grateful. Miracles are on the way and Spirit is by your side.

- You can create success in the material world by working hard and being smart, but if you're not authentic within that success, the experience will eventually be unsatisfying.
- Your soul has its own lane, but you are probably tempted to switch lanes in order to conform to others' ideas about what you should do and experience. However, anything that isn't true to who you are will be very hard to sustain.
- When the small self is open to hearing the soul, it serves as the soul's paintbrush.
- Journaling helps you remain open and present instead of becoming distracted, so it is a good tool for keeping your fears about the future and past at bay.

4

THE UNCHARTED JOURNEY

When the old ways of operating aren't working for you anymore, you're called to a journey. And when life is, on the surface, working just fine, as it was for me after my "rebranding," you can still be called to that journey so that you can live more authentically, with greater purpose and meaning.

Has your life taken a turn that has you lost and frustrated because you have tried and tried to be authentic and embody harmony and abundance, but the universe seems to be reflecting back to you chaos and scarcity? Call it a midlife crisis or a crisis of faith—or call it the beginning of a journey into the uncharted. This is your opportunity to write a much more meaningful and fulfilling story for yourself. Being in the uncharted places lends itself to reinvention, evolution, and an entirely new story of who you are and what your life is about.

THE HEROINE'S JOURNEY

To help you begin seeing your life story as a journey toward greater authenticity and power, you might want to watch some movies about journeys of self-transformation. You can start to see how a journey is really as much about what happens inside you as well as what happens outside of you. I find movies very helpful for getting in touch with what I'm going through and reflecting on my own challenges and how I'm handling them.

Many movies depict some version of the classic hero's journey, in which a hero decides to venture forth into unfamiliar lands, aided by allies and fortunate to have magical tools that can help him out when things get too hairy. The hero discovers strengths he didn't know he had. He's also forced to face some of his weaknesses and acknowledge them so they don't get him into serious trouble. In the end, he has a sense of mastery and achievement, but he has also come to be humbled by this challenging experience. He has transformed. Hero's journeys are at the center of *Star Wars, The Hobbit, How to Train Your Dragon,* and the Harry Potter books and movies, just to name a few. This hero's journey is a story template famously identified and explored by mythologist Joseph Campbell, and I know it's familiar to a lot of you.

A lesser-known story template is the heroine's journey, featured in movies such as *Wild* and *Frozen,* and it's a little different from the hero's journey. It's an *inward* journey of self-discovery that takes you deeper and deeper inside yourself to find your strengths and weaknesses and the inner resources you need to face challenges in your life. You might go somewhere, like on a hike or to a private spot in a remote area, or you might, like me, end up going to a hospital room to take it (I hope not!). In this kind of journey, you have to take yourself out of ordinary life, do some hard work, and then, finally, you can emerge transformed. Any magical rings, swords, or invisibility cloaks will have to be found inside of you—and fortunately, there are plenty of them there. You may have no idea what you will find inside to give you courage and power when you take this journey of internal exploration.

My recent hero's journey was arduous but absolutely worth taking. I ventured out onto a new career path and returned from it wiser and more comfortable inside my own skin. I had allies and tools, and I returned triumphant, having achieved success. But I also took a heroine's journey inward into the uncharted places within me. It was a journey I was forced into, because I couldn't think or strategize my way out of the fact that I was not living according to my soul's desires. I had to go inward, connect with Spirit, and begin to overcome my fears. That was the first step in my becoming who I needed to be to live the life of success and authenticity I yearned for—and it was an important one. Like every heroine's journey, mine was one of inward spiraling, discovering, illuminating, and healing the inner dragons of doubt and shame, returning them to their true forms of confidence and honest pride. I had to face what was distorting my vision of the world and my part in it. The uncharted journey is a quest to recover and retrieve the lost or broken parts of the self to be called back into wholeness. (Yes, I thought I had fully owned those parts of myself and incorporated them into my life, but as I explained earlier, it turned out I really hadn't, so I betrayed my gifts very quickly once I felt I was being judged and rejected and I got scared.)

As I lay in that hospital bed, not only did I get clarity about what I want to do with my career, which was helpful, to be sure, but I had to do a lot of inner work. Although I had taken a heroine's journey before (you may take them several times in your life), this one forced me to dig deep and find my strength and bravery to say no to ridicule and judgment no matter what. I emerged able to fully recommit to staying in my lane, answering the call of my soul.

The journey into the uncharted takes you deep into the place where your small self and soul can align and merge into the whole self. Integration happens. Because of that, the changes you want to make have sticking power. It's much easier to stay in your lane because you have made changes on the inside and become more authentic, more you.

A PLACE FOR SELF-REFLECTION

On the journey to the uncharted, you'll need to quiet your mind and reduce distractions so you can sense your soul and Spirit. You need a place for self-reflection, whether it's a physical place you retreat to or the time and space in which to unplug from distractions and get in touch with your soul and Spirit, entering into the Realm of Spirit that feels like home and provides a sense of safety and relief.

You could go on a short retreat, such as a weekend getaway that you spend in nature and in a nice empty room, cabin, or condo you share with no one but your dog! Virginia Woolf famously expressed this idea in *A Room of One's Own*. Art historian and critic Jacqueline Moss says it's important to have a space like this where you are "free to discover and rehearse a new version of [yourself] . . . a place of creative incubation." I agree, but maybe you have to attend to much in your life, so you have to do your inner journeying work in increments—20 minutes here, a day there, a couple of hours there. Whenever you consciously choose to go inward on this journey of discovery and transformation, avoid distractions so you can stay fully present and not have your small self fall asleep again.

Like the butterfly in the chrysalis, do what you can to take your time with the co-creative work you're called to do. You don't want to emerge before your wings are ready to unfold, flap, and take you aloft. If you are not ready to make big decisions while you're on this journey, listen to your instincts. You may have more evolving to do. Find space and time for quiet self-reflection in private.

In our culture, it's hard to "unplug." There's a lot of shaming about tuning in to your own needs—what some people call "navel-gazing." *Chop-chop, hurry up, we've got to move—now! What are you doing? Are you being productive and contributing? Did you stop to rest? Who do you think you are, resting?* I'm sure the chatterbox in your head has unleashed a string of anxiety-provoking thoughts like those many times! We all feel overstimulated and rushed, but our soul knows we are exactly where we are meant to be. If it has pulled you into uncharted territory and forced a heroine's journey onto you, it knows what it's doing.

YOUR STORY, YOUR JOURNEY

As you reflect on your experiences throughout this journey and notice your feelings and your thoughts about everything that you are going through at a time of great change, your story about your life and who you are is going to change. It's good for the small self to find a way of telling the story to yourself and others to make sense of it. You want it to be a story of you emerging into your most authentic self, with all sorts of lost aspects of who you are integrated back into your awareness. Maybe your story will end up going something like this: "I was so afraid to be myself, but I grew so weary of feeling like I had to keep pretending I was something I wasn't that I got sick from exhaustion. I began to pray; I surrendered to the experience and sailed into uncharted waters. I faced a few dragons, but I tamed them. I trusted in Spirit, and suddenly miracles started showing up. And I began to change, reclaiming parts of myself and learning how to be the new me. I emerged having integrated the past into a self that will never forget my own power and my own value."

After taking a journey into the uncharted, I promise you will have a tale to tell. Speak your truth about the transformation you experienced and how you came to return home. The story of your own journey could be a memoir, or writings about your experiences that are confined to your journal, or stories that you tell other people in a support group, in a public space, or on your blog. You might take the emotional truths of your story and some of the details and work them into a song (as I often do) or a dance.

Or your story may simply influence how you go about doing what you do every day—and quietly inspire others who observe you and how you live authentically. Your journey will have set you free to write a different story, one that is true to who you are.

What do you want to claim for yourself—or reclaim—so you can become the person you need to be to live the life you want to live? What, if any, fears are stopping you? If those fears have gotten in the way in the past, and you're afraid of meeting dragons on the road as you explore who you can become and what you can create for yourself, I have good news. You're going to learn some dragon-training strategies that will help tremendously.

Exercise: How Do You Tell Your Story?

Do you know that most of us don't realize that who we are today is a result of who we were? The way we self-define actually either supports us or thwarts us as we lead with the stories of our small self. In order to connect with the power source of Spirit we need to learn to "wear our stories loosely."

The purpose of this exercise is to help you see what binds you to old stories that aren't real for you anymore, to reinforce the stories that are still supportive, and to free you to explore what new stories you could write for yourself to experience.

In this exercise I invite you to explore the many ways you have defined yourself. I encourage you to "Know Thyself," which was the inscription at the ancient temple of Delphi. It's important to be without judgment and approach this with curiosity. This is not an easy process, so don't think too much about it; just let it flow from the deepest part of you.

There are 15 questions to answer about love, fear, sex, money, and God. After you work through all the questions once, I suggest you return once a month to see what has shifted within you: if you've changed, and if the outer conditions of your life have changed too, or if your perspective on your conditions has changed since you began working with this book.

When you get to the visualization part of the exercise, let your imagination be playful. Everything that comes up is correct. Don't try to control it, just let it flow, even if feels bizarre. This part of the exercise is symbolic; everything in it means something. After you've done the exercise, you can look up the meanings of the symbols on the Internet: type in "symbolic meaning of a pine tree" or "symbolic meaning of an elephant" and see what you discover.

1. What event or events have led to your core ideas about Love? What story do you tell about Love? Is it still true for you today? Write it down.
2. Now imagine this story about Love is an environment you inhabit. Allow your imagination to show you a place that represents Love. What does that place look like? Write down any details you think are pertinent. For example, you could be looking at a forest, or a swamp, or a beautiful meadow, or a busy town. You are the one observing the place. Write down what you see.
3. If you could write a new story for yourself and Love, what would it be? Who would you need to become to tell that story? If that story were a place, what would the new place look like?
4. What event or events have led to your core ideas about Fear? What story do you tell about Fear? Is it still true for you today? Write it down.
5. Now imagine this story about Fear is an environment you inhabit. Allow your imagination to show you a place that represents Fear. What does that place look like? Write down what you see.
6. If you could write a new story for yourself about Fear, what would it be? Who would you need to become to tell that story? If that story were a place, what would the new place look like?
7. What event or events have led you to your core ideas about Sex? What story do you tell yourself about Sex? Is it still true for you today? Write it down.
8. Now imagine this story about Sex is an environment you inhabit. Allow your imagination to show you a place that represents Sex. What does that place look like? Write down what you see.

9. If you could write a new story for yourself about Sex, what would it be? Who would you need to become to tell that story? If that story were a place, what would the new place look like?
10. What event or events have led you to your core ideas about Money? What story do you tell yourself about Money? Is it still true for you today? Write it down.
11. Now imagine this story about Money is an environment you inhabit. Allow your imagination to show you a place that represents Money. What does that place look like? Write down what you see.
12. If you could write a new story for yourself about Money, what would it be? Who would you need to become to tell that story? If that story were a place, what would the new place look like?
13. What event or events have led you to your core ideas about God (Source, Spirit, Higher Power, etc.)? What story do you tell yourself about God? Is it still true for you today? Write it down.
14. Now imagine this story about God is an environment you inhabit. Allow your imagination to show you a place that represents God. What does that place look like? Write down what you see.
15. If you could write a new story for yourself about your relationship with God (by many names), what would it be? Who would you need to become to tell that story? If that story were a place, what would the new place look like?

How you tell your story defines the Map you already have. The new story you write leads you into a new life beyond your wildest dreams.

Traveler's Notes

- The uncharted journey you are on (whether you wanted to take it or not!) is not necessarily a hero's journey that is external, although it can be. It is predominantly a heroine's journey that is internal.
- The internal heroine's journey is one of self-discovery, in which you quell your fears, find your strengths and weaknesses and inner resources, and transform yourself.
- Changes you make in your life after taking a journey to the uncharted will stick because going there and integrating what you've discovered ensures you will have evolved into the person you need to be.
- When you feel scared and uncertain, quiet your mind, reduce distractions, and "phone home": check in with Spirit, using your intuition and spiritual practices for opening a channel of communication.
- Don't rush the self-evolution. It takes time for a caterpillar to transform into a butterfly in the chrysalis.
- Begin to imagine what you want to claim for yourself and co-create for yourself. When your motivation is the highest good for all, miracles happen quickly and effortlessly.
- If fears are getting in your way, which happens for most of us, you need to learn to overcome them by "taming your dragons"—owning your personal power and trusting yourself to use that power wisely and ethically.

5

ABOUT THOSE DRAGONS . . .

As you stand there ready to embark on your journey inward into the uncharted, you and I need to have a little talk about those dragons.

When I say "dragon," what comes up in your mind? Maybe you think dragons are dangerous and horrible. Lots of people think that. But everyone's got a dragon within and it's not going away—because the dragon is an essential part of you: your personal power. Who would want to lose that?

What if you were to engage the dragon, like the flying dragons in the movie *Avatar*? Imagine a majestic, strong, beautiful beast that you could partner with and train to serve you as an ally so that both of you end up serving the greater good. Imagine you find your sense of confidence, faith, and purpose has grown beyond what you ever could have envisioned for yourself. Wouldn't it be fun to ride a dragon and soar above the ocean and through the clouds? What would it mean to have conquered your fears and be riding a brilliant fire-breathing creature fully empowered with wisdom, the fire of transformation, and the brilliant and soft light of curiosity?

And what if your dragon turns out to be a cute little beast like the dragon babies in the *Shrek* movies, merrily flying around and causing a bit of mischief but no serious harm? What if your fears became so small and amusing you could actually laugh at them? What would your life be like?

It's natural to fear the unfamiliar, and traditionally dragons are feared because we can't control them—kind of like our fears, which get away from us. We fear our fear; that's understandable. We fear our anger too, because that's hard to control. But fear and anger awaken us to the true nature of dragons: they represent our own power. When you feel fear or anger and want to run, that's when you need to go within and claim that power for yourself.

Spirit wants us to be empowered, but many of us don't trust ourselves not to screw up! We're afraid of what might happen if we climbed aboard a dragon, so we lock that creature up in a cave or hide it in the basement, where it goes mad and becomes cruel and refuses to help us in any way, breathing fire on us if we dare to face it. It hoards power, like Smaug, the greedy dragon in *The Hobbit* that can't possibly have enough gold trinkets and coins in its pile of riches that it guards fiercely.

And what feeds the dragon? Everything we don't like about ourselves and want to deny, like greed and selfishness, that we shove out of our consciousness and into the shadows of our psyche. With nothing else to eat, and nowhere to go, the dragon has no choice but to swallow it all—and then he's burping and farting fire all over the place! So much for being the kind, compassionate, spiritual people we like to think we are. We get ugly, snarky, and mean and take advantage of other people or cut them down when we get jealous, and then feel horribly guilty. That kind of behavior is the fire of the dragon, and it's very destructive. No wonder we want to deny or try to slay the dragon. It's not happening! But that's okay, because we can *train* him—that's right, just like the boy hero in a movie you might remember called *How to Train Your Dragon*.

You'll work with this dragon in the process of your journey inward to the uncharted. This dragon, your personal power, gets acknowledged in the Realm of Mind, and then in the Realm of Light its fiery breath illumines what you're doing and what you have to acknowledge about yourself and integrate into your life whether you like it or not. In the Realm of Energy, you climb on that dragon's back and direct it. Finally, in the Realm of Form, your personal power has become integrated, and you're able to be the person you want to be—genuinely kind, understanding, compassionate, courageous, and powerful. What a wonderful ally the dragon can turn out to be!

But can we be trusted atop this wild creature of our own power and feel confident we won't mess up and cause the dragon to fly around erratically, setting afire everything we see, like the creatures in the movie before the boy came to understand and work with them?

You are here to use your Spirit-given personal power for co-creation. You *can* handle this power without hurting yourself or others. But to do that, you have to understand the nature and origins of the fears that make you lock up your dragon—or let it fly about randomly starting fires and destroying things! Tame your fears and you start to train your dragon. You acknowledge, access, and responsibly use your personal power.

SELF-CENTERED FEARS

Fear is a tricky companion that robs you of your true power if you try to deny it out of embarrassment or shame. It shuts down your intuition and your ability to reconnect with your soul, know Spirit, and co-create what you long to experience. I don't care how many workshops you attend, how many books you read, or how much tapping you do, you can't co-create the life you want when that trickster fear is on the loose and running the show.

Fear leads you into the fun house distortion of reality that every one of us knows intimately. Your perceptions of yourself and the situations you find yourself in become twisted as this trickster comes onto your path. It will test you and provide false evidence appearing as real. When outer conditions appear to be misaligned with what you desire or you step into unknown territory and forget to ask for help in navigating the uncharted, fear shows up in one form or another. Its presence challenges you to wake up.

Now, what I'm talking about here isn't the rational fear you experience when you're truly in danger. I'm talking about fear that is rooted in the small self—fear that I learned to call in the early days of my recovery "self-centered fear." The small self fears being hurt emotionally, not getting what it wants, losing something it cares about, not belonging, or being ridiculed. Self-centered fears keep you from exercising your personal power, and they get activated when you're feeling disconnected from your soul and from Spirit.

I notice self-centered fears in my own life when I get triggered and start stumbling around in a bout of temporary spiritual amnesia. Sure, my small self's fears have diminished over time, but I can still freak out when the bills pile up higher than I expect. *Oh no! We're going to lose it all and I'll end up a bag lady!* It's totally irrational, but I go there anyway! Sometimes I fall into the fear that if I'm too much myself, I'll end up being punished or ostracized. Where are those fears coming from? Well, many of them are the same self-centered fears my mother struggled with—more on that later. Let me just say that my experiences have taught me this important truth: if you can manage those self-centered fears, turn them around, and trust the power within to lead you forward rather than backward, miracles can and do happen.

Practicing radical acceptance, compassion, and self-love softens self-centered fears. But the only way to get back into a state of being where I can practice all that is if I awaken my Observing Self, realize that I'm in a landscape of fear, and get myself back to the safe place of love and support that I'm calling the Realm of Spirit.

To find the magic on your soul's Map, you have to break the habit of giving in to self-centered fears. When you surrender fully to Spirit, saying with full gratitude and fullness of heart, "Thank you!" and trusting that you are being lovingly cared for, you will release those fears. Then when you see the dragon, you can say, "Hello!" and chuck it under the chin, where it likes to be petted. You have a new relationship to your personal power. It's not so scary after all. You can trust yourself because you're honest about who you are and what you're struggling with, and you make peace with the fact that you'll always have work to do on yourself. Feed that dragon love, compassion, and kindness. Laugh with it and play with it. Then it will happily become your ally instead of a guarded, crabby monster within you that belches fire because its stomach is upset!

Self-centered fears are impossible to erase altogether because let's face it, you're never going to be perfect. So what? While you're evolving into the person you want to be, you can quiet those self-centered fears and start wielding personal power wisely and responsibly. Regularly "phone home" and check in with the Divine, orienting yourself in the Realm of Spirit. You *can* be trusted to co-create something new. You can climb aboard your dragon and sing with joy as you fly around, playing with this power. Wanton destructiveness? No, that's not you. Don't be afraid of yourself and what you might do if you broke some rules and left behind familiar ways. Fly free atop your dragon!

WHAT ARE YOU AFRAID OF, REALLY?

Do you know what you most fear? Often, what you fear isn't so scary after all once you actually face it and name it. In fairy tales, knowing the name of the goblin or creature who is tormenting you gives you power over it. (I talk about this at length in my last book, *The Map*.) If you're a fan of the Harry Potter stories, you'll remember that unlike so many magical beings who knew about the evil Voldemort, Harry refused to call him "He who must not be named." He spoke the name of his nemesis—and that led to him ultimately vanquishing that snake-nosed villain. Maybe if you faced your own fear and gave it a name, you too would feel a sense of power and actually sense that you *can* conquer the fear. Is your fear called "I don't belong" or "I'm not good enough"? Or is it "There's not enough!" or "Not allowed to shine"?

One of the fears many people share is the fear of admitting just how afraid and vulnerable they are! We take ourselves, and our fears, very seriously and are ashamed or angry at ourselves for our lack of courage. But the courage is there! You may not feel it now, and you may have been unable to access it at times in the past, but I promise you it's there. You just have to get used to calling it up.

Life is a series of challenges to our courage. Most of the time we forget we have the capacity to enter the unknown with courage and curiosity. Why? Because we fall out of practice! When you look around, there's a lot of support for fear, even in the form of advertisements reminding you that if you don't have a certain possession or look a certain way, you're worthless and you don't belong, so pull out your credit card—now! News services sell fear; so do politicians. Fear can stimulate you into irrational action—like buying whatever junk someone is selling you.

When you are feeling paralyzed by fear, use the following exercise to access your Observing Self, separate from your fear, and reclaim your power. It will take you about 15 minutes. Just as with all the exercises in this book, do it in a quiet, private place without distractions. Sit comfortably and focus on your breathing to turn the volume down on your small self's incessant chatter and open a channel to your soul's wisdom. Listen to meditation music if you find it helpful for shifting out of the "yadda yadda" mind-set of distraction. Afterward, journal about what you learned and experienced.

Exercise: Get On That Winged Creature!

Sit comfortably and breathe deeply and slowly, inhaling to a count of six. Gently exhale, and allow your body to relax. Keep breathing slowly and deeply, and notice where in your body you are feeling fear. Is it in your chest? Your throat? Shoulders?

Now ask yourself, "When I feel this way, where am I?"

(In other words, if this feeling were a place you were temporarily inhabiting rather than an emotion you identified with, what would you be looking at?)

Notice what the place looks like as you allow your mind to reveal it to you. It could be a swamp, an old warehouse, a charred forest—whatever it is, trust that your unconscious knows exactly how to show you what you need to see. You may only get a glimpse of a landscape, or you might see a constant image with lots of detail. If you're not very visual as a thinker, you'll just know what the place is. You might get a flash of an image and some descriptive words that tell you where you are emotionally—"in a stifling, hot schoolroom from my childhood," or whatever it is.

Notice how this place is not you, but you are the one looking at it. Then, when you are able to shift from feeling the stress to looking at the landscape that represents the stress, pay special attention to the distance you sense between your Observing Self and the place.

Call on a winged creature now to come to empower you to leave this place. This is your dragon!

Don't try to force this—if a sleek green dragon is what you think you should see, but a chubby purple one appears, let it be what it wants. This process is about receiving images as opposed to creating them, so whatever shows up will be what you need to see.

Imagine yourself getting on the back of your dragon and flying high into the sky until all you see is blue surrounding you.

Now look down and see how large or small the original place is from this vantage point. Remain aware of being the observer of the scene rather than being in it.

Now allow your imagination to see this place you were just in as a place inside a snow globe, contained in a ball of glass, sitting in the hands of God, or Spirit, or the Divine—whatever name you give this loving Consciousness. Where are you in this scene?

Can the place in the snow globe affect you in any way now?

Compare your perspective now with how you felt when you began.

Would you make the same choices, behave the same way, or react the same in that place as opposed to outside it? Or would your choices and actions be different? If so, how?

Come back into ordinary awareness, and write about your experience.

Then choose a current life experience that causes you stress and describe how you feel, think, and deal with things while you're "in it," fully immersed in the stressful situation. What would happen if you were to awaken your Observing Self, the way you did in the exercise? How could your Observing Self help you?

IS FEAR TAKING YOU TO THE GHOSTLANDS?

One of the biggest challenges in overcoming self-centered fears is that when we're afraid, we're likely not in the present. In *The Map*, I talked about the Ghostlands, a metaphor for where we're trapped in thoughts or feelings about the past or future. Both future and past are the repositories of our fear and cause us much trouble in the present. We can't bring back yesterday nor change anything that has already happened, and the future's large promise or potential problems are not here either. The only power we have over those illusions is to bring our consciousness back to the present moment and get out of those Ghostlands, where nothing is real but the fear can be paralyzing.

The small self is like Chicken Little. It always has a story about how the sky is falling, when really it just got bonked on the head by a falling acorn. When the small self stops and pays attention to the present, it can remember it has a limited perspective and choose to awaken its higher awareness. It can phone home, and the soul self will wake up and sort things out.

Your fear today may simply be a shadow of an old memory of suffering. Can you identify how it feels in your body when you are afraid? Maybe you begin to feel nauseated, or you notice your hands are shaking, or you get light-headed and feel your face growing warm as you flush. Maybe you feel tension in your muscles in a certain part of your body. Fear feels real because it creates a physiological response in the Realm of Form. If you release it, using your mind and imagination to return to a calming state of being, your body will respond accordingly.

The next time you feel anxious or scared, stop yourself and pay attention to what you're feeling in your body. Be present with yourself and observe how you feel. When you do this, you're likely to notice that the physical response of fear starts fading and you begin thinking more clearly. You can decide if you want to focus on your breathing or do some other exercise to release the fear further, such as the Get On That Winged Creature exercise, or just go back to the situation you were in. You will have taken yourself out of the Ghostlands and put yourself back into the present moment, where you can use the Observer Self's perspective to ask yourself questions about your fear:

- How scared am I, on a scale of 1 to 10?
- Is the thing I'm fearing actually true right now?
- What else is true? Is there another truth here, one that isn't so scary?
- Who would I need to become to experience this situation differently and not be afraid?

It's okay if you don't know the answers. As you work through the process of co-creative evolution on this journey into the uncharted, you're going to discover strengths and abilities that allow you to become the person you need to be to triumph over self-centered fears.

Fear of an uncertain future is part of being human. But very often, our fears are exaggerated. Reminders of experiences we've had in the past trigger self-centered fears, and worries about an uncertain future naturally scare us. Courage doesn't mean the absence of fear. It means choosing not to turn away from the scary uncharted places in spite of the vulnerability you might feel in the fear. The goal is progress, not perfection. If you freak out for an hour today, it doesn't mean you're not courageous. Just breathe and say, "Thank you, Spirit. I know you're here. I've got this." If your small self is whispering fiercely, "No you don't," just keep saying, "Thank you" and affirming your courage.

Although I'm an intuitive, I can't know for certain exactly what will happen tomorrow or in the months to come. I get scared too! I shared with you earlier how I allowed my own self-centered fears to take me hostage and keep me on the run. But when fear sets in, I orient myself on the Map of my soul and plant myself firmly in the Realm of Spirit. I feel safe, because I know I'm being protected, and I open up to receive Spirit's messages clearly. And I say, "Thank you, Spirit." I feel gratitude because it reminds me that ultimately it's all good. There's discomfort along the way, but the sky is *not* falling. The future is always uncharted, filled with a myriad of potentials and possibilities, and the best way to ensure you will engage it with power and clarity is by drawing your attention to the present—because that's where you find your co-creative powers.

In Alcoholics Anonymous (AA), they teach the concept of living one day at a time, suggesting that anyone can live present to anything that could occur in one day: "God only gives you what you can handle on any given day." Yet so many of us fall into the cha-cha dance of "I'm awake! Wow, this world is magical and all is well all the time. What can I co-create with Spirit today?" and "Snorrrrr, oh my god, there's not enough, the sky is falling, they are going to take away what's mine! I'm not good enough!" When we slow down, get quiet, immerse ourselves in the present moment, the small self and the soul self merge. Then the small self's fears about the future and about the limitations of today grow quieter. You don't go deaf to your small self, but it loses its ability to keep you from accessing your personal power.

I have made my living successfully glimpsing the potentials and probabilities of the future as a way to help guide my clients to make better decisions or to confirm what they already know. But I moved into coaching in order to help my clients consciously embody the experience they desire and become the people they want to be—the people their souls call them to be—rather than repeat the past (which we do when we're on automatic pilot). To achieve the successes my clients are aiming for, that their souls are calling them to, they have to slow down, unplug, and remain present even when their self-centered fears overtake them.

Do you believe now that you can do the same? Trust me—you can! If there are vestiges of fear clinging to you as you look at your soul's Map, you can experience that life on this planet as fun, a game to be enjoyed as long as you're playing it.

FEARS FROM THE PAST

Many of your self-centered fears aren't even yours. Some of them you have absorbed through continual exposure to all the bad things happening in the world. Don't plug in 24/7 to what's happening with everyone else and around the globe! Turn it off for stretches, because our nervous systems weren't designed to handle the excess stimulation. And keep in mind that some of your self-centered fears were inherited from the adults who raised you and guided you when you were young.

We're all affected by the stories we heard growing up and by experiences in our formative years between birth and age six, when we were constantly downloading information about the world. The fears we developed in that time can remain in us all our lives. You may be aware of these inherited patterns in yourself.

Yet there are also ancestral patterns of thought and belief that we inherit unawares. These are transferred to us energetically and even genetically—new research is revealing more and more about how they're passed down via DNA—and their effect on us is profound. We internalize the patterns energetically, and then we end up attracting and manifesting more situations that resonate with our fear, reflecting it.

This was the case for Claire, a student in one of my workshops. As I tuned in to the spirits in the room, I connected to a group of very chatty dead people who couldn't wait to speak to their loved ones. An Italian Catholic mother and a grandmother came through to apologize for putting Claire down. They expressed that they had been wrong to do that, and they knew they had caused Claire such turmoil because of her gifts as a psychic and a healer. They said that they'd done this because of their strong religious beliefs while they were still alive. They were very specific in their messages so Claire would know it was them.

She broke down in tears, saying she had worked for a long time as an intuitive but had never felt safe doing so. Over the years as her gifts developed and more and more people wanted to work with her, you might think she would have developed more confidence and comfort with her choice to do intuitive work. Instead, she became more conflicted about her abilities. To make matters worse, she had an ongoing expectation that she would never be accepted by anyone who loved her. Consequently, she became quite isolated and stopped doing the work and engaging in spiritual activities. She became an accountant and did well in her career, but always felt like she was "missing something." When I met her, she was only just beginning to reclaim her intuitive abilities after being shut down for so long.

Claire said both her mother and her grandmother were also highly intuitive but were told intuition was evil and would cause them to go to hell—in fact, her grandmother was severely beaten by her own father because of her psychic abilities and her desire to share them, and so she beat Claire's mother too when she showed signs of this "abhorrent trait of the devil." The legacy of belief was passed down woman to woman until each woman denied her own capacity for this essential connection and gave in to fear instead. These women were strong, opinionated, vibrant, and even tough on the outside when they were alive, but in the hidden recesses of their psyches, they expected to be abused.

When we accept a story about ourselves, even if at some level we believe it to be wrong, there is always a low-grade anxiety about what is true or not true. Without realizing it, we sabotage ourselves in order to be in alignment with the original story. In this way, fears from the past can prevent us from being all we can be.

The universe will always reflect back whatever we repeat and reinforce over time. To change our lives, we have to evolve within and become the people we need to become.

"JUST TELL ME WHAT I WANT TO HEAR ABOUT THE FUTURE!"

As I said, although as an intuitive I've seen true and accurate details of people's futures and have built my reputation on this, these days I'm cautious about discussing the future with my clients when they are grasping for certainty about it. I always say readings are guideposts, not hitching posts. Knowledge is power, yet I believe it's much more beneficial for all of us to understand how to become the most empowered version of ourselves in the now than to spend too much energy thinking about what could be.

Like everyone, though, as I mentioned earlier, I can get freaked out too. I just want to *know* that the future will be a place where my hard work will have "paid off" and I will be free. The game can be very scary and frustrating at times! Yet it's only when I remain in the now, wearing the world as a loose garment, unattached to outcomes and in a state of curiosity and gratitude, that I know that very freedom intimately. I lighten up and trust in Spirit. The soul's Map comes to life, and it's all good.

A few years ago, a colleague of mine, Robert Ohotto, a brilliant soul-contract astrologer wise beyond his years, predicted I would leave my publisher. He said this would happen because I would need to have a different experience within which to evolve. I wasn't ready to hear that emotionally and didn't understand what he was implying. I had found a home in Hay House, was given countless opportunities to shine and to share my gifts, yet even though I had found a place where I belonged, I had not yet belonged to myself. Of course, my friend the intuitive was right.

As I said before, we may take several journeys in our lives, and there are times when we will find ourselves in uncharted territories whether we want to be there or not. I had been in such denial, resisting my gift for years, and even though I'd made very good progress toward erasing my fear of being seen as "out there," it was still lingering. I was still hungry for legitimacy and thought a mainstream publisher would give it to me. But to find the legitimacy that was missing, I needed to find it in myself. At this point in my life, I was like the Scarecrow, Cowardly Lion, and Tin Man looking for someone to give me what I already had within. My challenge was to discover it and reclaim it.

Even so, leaving my publisher to go find legitimacy "out there" somewhere outside myself on my hero's journey of adventure was an amazing experience! The relationships I formed are still strong and vibrant today regardless of my later choice to return "home" to Hay House. During this time, I proved to myself that I was as good as other authors who had achieved the same stature. But I quickly learned that my outer accomplishments were not the issue and never had been. This journey into uncharted waters wasn't about financial gain, accolades, or any other type of outer acceptance—although I achieved all those too. I thought I was manifesting a different reality, one that was more authentic to who I was or wanted to be. But the more I settled into my new situation, the more my spirit became restless. My small self wasn't any more certain or safe. Something had to change, and that something was *me.*

Are you feeling that way—yearning to listen to your soul instead of playing it safe? Don't get ahead of yourself and rush to make your life better and change your circumstances before you've done the work you need to do within. Don't go back into the past, to the familiar Map, thinking you'll do the same thing again and achieve different results. The future starts inside you, as you begin your process of evolution within.

THE FUTURE BEGINS TODAY, INSIDE YOU

I had seen this story of being inauthentic and ending up outside of your lane play out often with my clients and friends, but I couldn't see it in myself! We try to resist the call to evolve because we're afraid of what we'll lose. What I've learned as a medium conversing with those on the other side is that they're urging us to belong to Spirit and to ourselves first before concerning ourselves with others. They want us to write new stories, and that means venturing into the uncharted places. They are asking us to face our fears and trust Spirit—to trust the true nature of abundance, our infinite potential and inherent and essential goodness.

When you journey within and face the parts of yourself you were afraid to see before, you'll start to realize just how deeply you have underestimated yourself. The soul is free of all the fear-based, limited notions of the small self that constantly says, "I can't. Not me." It can see your weaknesses as strengths, and it isn't afraid to bring your strengths to light. If people become jealous, so be it—that's about them, not you. If they reject you, it's their loss—other friends and allies will take their place in your tribe.

Become the person you need to be to bring about the future you would like to experience. You do that within, by visiting and exploring the uncharted places on the Map. There, you find you aren't so small after all.

It's hard to accept this at first. You have to "try on" the person you want to be, who is brave and extraordinary. You have to make that experience real to you in the now. Who will you become if you step into uncharted waters? What will you discover about yourself if you face the self-centered fears that have held you back and prevented you from taking risks?

Let's look at two common self-centered fears: the fear of not belonging and the fear of being inadequate (and consequently being shamed). These two lie within everyone—and block our access to the treasures of our souls. Get them out of your way, and you can regain your personal power.

YOU HAVE ALLIES!

Too many people hide parts of themselves in the shadows of their psyches because they fear being cast out from the community. The fear of not belonging, of being rejected, is a primal one we have inherited, embedded in our DNA. Even introverts and loners need to be with others to some degree—and they long for acceptance. Many of our self-centered fears are, on closer inspection, just variations on the fear of not belonging.

This fear was even stronger for me growing up than it was for many. My mother, who was Jewish, came of age in Nazi Germany, where you were killed for being a Jew, a gypsy, a homosexual—anything that did not fit the Aryan standard. Having lost her own mother to a bomb, my mom was raised by her wealthy Jewish grandparents, and then when she was no longer safe there, she was hidden by a Christian family, who later adopted her. My mother believed she would never be safe unless she could hide anything that would make her different.

My mother escaped from Germany, moved to Canada, met my father, and had my sister and me. My Serbian father changed our last name from Bogdanovic to Baron. (Given that his family had existed in the reign of King Peter of Yugoslavia, we grew up believing we were titled aristocracy, although now we think that just meant the family had a lot of pigs and cows.) My parents raised us as Christians and my mother completely hid her Jewish origins even from her husband. Together, they created new lives, new titles and personas, and stories about who they were. They spent their lives making sure the four of us "belonged" and "were safe."

When my father lost the family fortune at the age of 75, he went from being sharp and brilliant to an old man with dementia—as if overnight. I am convinced the daily terror of financial insecurity and the drastic change in our lifestyle caused the brain tumor that killed my mom a year after my father died of a stroke. When we were dealing with her meager estate, my sister and I realized she had died one year before she would have become completely penniless.

Did my parents' internal fear of not being accepted and safe manifest in the physical world as evidence that they *were not* accepted and safe? My father was ambitious and brilliant but always wanted bigger, faster, higher; to please his business partners and gain entrance to their billionaire worlds, he put up everything he owned as security, only to have his faith in them betrayed in too many ways to count. He was never going to change the way they saw him as "other." Meanwhile, although my mom had wanted to go to medical school, she opted out because my father was the breadwinner. Being a stay-at-home mother felt like a safe choice for the family, yet she became dependent on him financially—and her sense of safety turned out to be an illusion. I fiercely love my parents, who tried so hard to create a sense of safety and belonging for themselves and their children. And I understand them now in ways I never thought possible. But because I love them, I can learn from them today and look without shame or embarrassment at how their self-centered fears held them back from their power to co-create the security and belonging they so desperately wanted for themselves.

We all hold ourselves back and sabotage ourselves, and there is no shame in it. But the past does not have to repeat. You have the power to co-create a new reality in new and extraordinary ways.

YOU ARE WORTHY!

While I was writing this chapter, Fred urged me to go back and watch *Wayne's World* and reacquaint myself with Wayne and Garth, so I did. I'd forgotten how sweet and vulnerable they are, and how they're so relentlessly optimistic about their lives that you just want to hug them. They just wanna rock and roll! In one scene, they get to meet one of their idols, rock star Alice Cooper, and when he invites them to hang out with him and his band, Wayne and Garth become starstruck, drop to their knees, and kowtow, declaring, "We're not worthy! We're not worthy!" Oh my god, don't we all do that sometimes when we're faced with the possibility of stepping out of our stories of being ordinary? We see the greatness and success we long for reflected outside of us, and we don't know how to own it. We just freak out, screaming, "Ack! I'm not worthy!"

Well, guess what? You *are* worthy. We all are. We are powerful co-creators when we say no to our fear and yes to our personal power. So why do we feel the need to hide our light, apologize for ourselves, and compare ourselves negatively with others, shouting, "We're not worthy"? Because we don't want to be rejected—it's so painful! If we aren't humble enough, people might think we are arrogant and start hating us and ostracizing us—that's the fear. The fear of not belonging and the fear of being unworthy are closely related.

But again, all of us are "good enough"—and none of us are responsible for anyone else's jealousy. Jealousy is all about believing "I can't have what she has." Sometimes that's a lie people tell themselves—but we're not responsible for their beliefs. Sometimes it's true—we have more, at least in the Realm of Form, for now. But denying what we have to make jealous people feel better just reinforces a belief that to be happy and contented, you have to have things others may have but you lack.

Inspiring other people to step into their personal power and become who they want to be, and experience what they long to experience, happens when you let your light shine. To do that, you have to recognize that it is light—that what you think of as a weakness may also be seen as a strength. And whatever you are still working on transforming within yourself, remember that you have value as you are, right now.

You are enough. There is enough. This is the real truth.

ANYTHING IS POSSIBLE

The small self has value but has to be right-sized in service to the soul and to Spirit. If you're going to co-create from a place of true, authentic power, your small self has to stop all its anxious chatter that hijacks your consciousness with worry that you won't count and that you won't be loved and accepted and supported, or that you need to have power over others to matter, to be important, to thrive.

When you fear there's not enough or that you're not enough, you go into panic mode, and there's no room for gratitude. You buy into your own powerlessness, become defensive, deny your role in creating your situation, and become overwhelmed by a scarcity mentality. You hoard, grow small, and become afraid to take chances. You stop trusting other people, your gut, and Spirit. Then the lying begins. You lie to yourself and others and push aside the awful feeling that you're being inauthentic. *You forget who you really are and what you came here to do!*

Blaming others doesn't help you make the shift into courage and recognizing the support of Spirit and your own soul working together. Blaming yourself and just trying to paddle as fast as you can as you tell yourself how stupid and inadequate you were keeps you stuck in the pain and suffering caused by your small self.

All this fear that keeps us small is understandable. It's been indoctrinated into us. We see the world as us against them. When we identify with *me* and not *we*, driven by human wants, and forget there's a greater spiritual viewpoint, then our fear takes over, we abdicate our personal power, and our dragons become destructive monsters stuck in the basement belching fire. We can make ourselves ill or even turn on the genes for serious disease when we hold on to fear and shame and keep our personal power at bay. Or we resent others and compete against them, or want to control them, or become small with jealousy.

But you don't have to do any of that if you work with the five interconnected realms of co-creation and train any dragons you find while doing this work so that you can take advantage of your personal power and not be crippled by fear. You've already learned much about the Realm of Spirit, our home base where you integrate small self and soul self into whole self and recognize that you are lovable and loved—that you are never alone. You know how to go there now; you know how to get in touch with your first sense, intuition, and orient yourself in the Realm of Spirit. Now it's time for you to learn about the other four realms and how they all intersect so you can begin the work of co-creative evolution that's the reason you are in the uncharted places in the first place. Anything is possible, and you don't have to be afraid anymore.

Traveler's Notes

- A "dragon" is a metaphor for your personal power, which you may fear because you do not feel capable of controlling it and using it wisely and ethically.
- Fear and anger can awaken you to the fact that you have power you don't always use the way you should. Tame your fears to start to train your dragon.
- Fear from the small self shuts down your intuition and your ability to reconnect with your soul, know Spirit, and co-create what you long to experience.
- Three common fears are admitting just how afraid and vulnerable we are, not belonging, and being unworthy of our power.
- Fear takes us out of the present and into the past and future as we remember old suffering or fear what might happen to us—or what we might not be able to experience.
- Some of our small self's fears are not even ours, but ones we inherited from our past or even our parents and grandparents.

- When we accept a story about ourselves even though at some level we believe it to be wrong, we unknowingly sabotage ourselves in order to be in alignment with the original story.
- The universe will always reflect back whatever we repeat and reinforce over time. To change our lives, we have to evolve within.
- We try to resist the call to evolve because we're afraid of what we'll lose.
- The small self has to be right-sized, in service to the soul and to Spirit.
- When we identify with *me* and not *we*, driven by human wants, and forget there's a greater spiritual viewpoint, small-self fears take over and we abdicate our personal power.
- Small-self fears dissolve when we practice compassion, radical self-acceptance, and gratitude, which take us back home to the Realm of Spirit.

PART II

THE FIVE REALMS OF CO-CREATION

6

HOW THE REALMS OF CO-CREATION ARE INTERCONNECTED

On the Map of the soul, there are five interconnected realms. The Realm of Spirit is a center hub that both transcends and infuses four other realms—Mind, Light, Energy, and Form. It unites them in the same way that the states are united into a country or the provinces are united as Canada. In the realms of Mind, Light, Energy, and Form, you are always in the Realm of Spirit as well. You might not realize it, however, because your small self falls into spiritual narcolepsy quite often and becomes oblivious to your connection to the great matrix—or Mind of All. Carl Jung called this "mind" the collective unconscious and said it exists within every individual's unconscious mind. Metaphysicist Edgar Cayce referred to it as the Akashic plane, where we can access information about past, present, and future nonlocally, because the rules of time and space do not apply. It is there, before you, at hand, whether you realize it or not. And it is a treasure chest of wisdom and potentiality!

Spirit is the quintessence, present in all things at all times, and all possibilities exist within the consciousness of Spirit. Although it is invisible to the naked eye and human perception when you're observing the world as consisting of distinct parts, like a machine, the Realm of Spirit makes itself obvious to you once you learn to align with it, dialogue with it, and decipher its messages. Spirit is your co-creative partner. Magic happens when you learn how to invoke Spirit, saying, "Thank you—thank you in advance for helping me!" That puts you firmly into the Realm of Spirit beyond the limited materialism of the Realm of Form.

The realms of co-creation are always interconnected and communicating, separated from each other only by their purpose. To live in sync with the longings of your soul, find magic in the uncharted places, and minimize your risk of unnecessary exposure to dragon fire, orient yourself in the Realm of Spirit as you've learned to do in Part I of this book before making decisions and reacting to what life presents. In this realm of magic, the Map of your soul lights up, you see the patterns you missed before, the uncharted places become visible, and you see all that is familiar as well. Everything is so much clearer!

But where should you go next from that center hub, where you experience the quintessence of all life that is Spirit? In the world of the senses, you might answer the question, "Where next and what next?" with lists and plans, research, and conversations with people you trust—all of which has value. I'm not asking you to close your eyes, say, "Spirit, whisk me away," and magically have all your decisions made for you. If you did that, you wouldn't be taking responsibility for yourself as a soul that has chosen to incarnate and have experiences through the constructs of the physical body and the individual persona that is you. You are in this game for now, and you must face whatever is before you, however scary it is at times. Fortunately, Spirit is with you, revealing itself through signs, messages, nature, and people. Don't forget that when you tune out distractions and tune in to your intuition, the messages come through much more loudly. Spirit's numinous presence will nudge you and guide you if you open to it by orienting yourself in the first of the five interconnected realms and pulling out the Map of your soul.

Now let's look more closely at the spiral path you will travel on your journey of inner discovery as you co-create a new reality for yourself. I know how tempting it is to go straight to the last realm, that of form, where energy manifests as matter and your dreams come true in ways that you can touch and see. The Realm of Form is where you find the house, the job, the partner, the healing you seek, the perfect opportunity, and the situation you would never have guessed would bring you tremendous joy. However, if you start there and ignore the spiritual realm and the workings of the Map of the soul, you can become very lost and travel far away from what you say you desire. That's what I was trying to do by rebranding myself as "only" a coach and intuitive strategist and denying my soul's calling to connect people with spirits who have crossed over as part of their own soul's process of deepening, growing, and expanding. You can also end up with exactly what you wanted, right down to the last detail, accompanied by other situations and circumstances that try your very soul or make you restless and discontented. Be careful what you wish for. Wish well from the Realm of Spirit before trying to manifest what you think you want. The essence is more important than the form.

It's easy to forget this. As soon as we come into this world as souls and take on a physical body, we become subject to the optical illusion of a five-sensory experience in the material world. We forget about the soul's Map and the realms we have to journey through in the process of co-creating the reality we desire. We need to be reminded so that we can do what we came here to do: engage in personal transformation and evolution, even as we co-create a better world and have fun doing it.

Yes, we're supposed to create and experience all of it—the laughter and the suffering—and wear the world loosely around our shoulders. It's much easier to do this when you remember you are not the only co-creator of reality, so while determination and planning are great, know that you will run up against obstacles and situations that are beyond your control. There are other agendas set in motion by others, by the larger group of sleepwalkers, by realities no longer in alignment with yours.

Also, your soul is much more powerful at this co-creating business than your small self is. It can have a very different agenda than your small self, and it always has more power because it is tapped into the energetic forces of the matrix. Spiritual narcolepsy, in which you forget about your soul and cut yourself off from access to its wisdom, makes it very hard to co-create what you desire.

Have you ever found yourself wondering, *How did I get back into another situation with a person like this when I swore I'd never do that again and I was vigilant about all the signs?* If so, remember, you don't control the universe. None of us is that powerful! Difficult people are out there, and they will show up in your life, and you can decide whether or not to engage them. It may be that what is before you was set in motion by others in the past or even by you (it takes time for form to respond to your intention to co-create something different). But if you seize on this opportunity to meet the needs of your soul on its journey, you will increase your ability to avoid similar situations in the future.

When things aren't going well and you have decisions to make, stop and enter the Realm of Spirit and pull out the Map of your soul. From there, you enter the first realm of co-creation, the Realm of Mind, and begin to transform within. That way, the energetic pull of people who trigger your old issues, and situations that mirror what's unresolved within you, will cease. The dragons will go to sleep and you can step around them, saying, "Been there, done that, and I've moved on." And that will be the truth—because you are in a realm where a process of co-creative evolution can begin.

FROM SPIRIT TO MIND

When I use my intuitive gifts to connect with the other side, I start in the Realm of Spirit—rather like dialing a number on my cell phone—but then quickly find myself in the Realm of Mind. The connection has been made and my intuition is bringing in messages from Spirit. I am seeing an image—let's say it's a cruise ship and palm trees—or I have a sensation of tightness somewhere in my body or energy field. Sometimes I connect to a personal memory that brings up a key word for me that will have meaning for the person I'm reading. My intuition works in many different ways. And I have my own interpretation of the messages I receive, but I will often describe what I'm experiencing in case my interpretation is off. The funny thing is sometimes what I see is literally accurate, while other times it's all metaphor and symbol. Spirit communicates in symbol, speaking to my mind through my consciousness, but then I have to interpret the messages here in the Realm of Mind.

I remember once when I was reading a woman, I saw a distinct image in my mind's eye of her house being blown up and an image of her husband attached to it. I felt the jolt in my body and felt the foundation being blown to bits. Then I saw an image of a new home built on solid foundations that she would love. So I cleared my throat and began to tell her what I thought I was seeing: that her husband was about to destroy their marriage and topple the foundations of her security, but then would rebuild their marriage better than before. I proceeded to explain in no uncertain terms that she needed to be prepared for what appeared to be a large explosion, but that she should not be afraid, for in the future everything would be, well, coming up roses! Before I got a chance to finish my interpretation of what I saw, she started laughing her head off. She told me her husband was a demolitions expert, and indeed the very next day he would be blowing up their house so they could build another one. I asked her what she thought of roses, and she replied that she loved them so much she was planning to plant large rosebushes all around the new structure. Always good to ask.

One of my other favorite stories to tell (and I think I told it in one of my earlier books) is about speaking to a large audience in the early days when I'd just started accessing my skill as a medium. A woman stood in front of me and I knew I was supposed to connect to her. I heard this shrill, high-pitched voice saying, "Lily, Lily, Lily," and I saw what appeared to be a short, round old woman—presumably Lily—wearing a fur coat. Then I saw an image of the woman's lingerie drawer. I was flooded with emotions of love and excitement coming from this spirit, and information about problems with the woman's feet. I looked at the woman I was reading and let her know her grandmother Lily was wanting to talk to her, described her wearing her fur coat, and asked, did she have something of Lily's she might have left behind in her lingerie drawer? Confused for a moment, the woman shook her head and then shrieked, "Oh my God, that's my hamster!" *Lily the hamster*—round? Fur coat? Get it? Apparently, the hamster sometimes hung out in the lingerie drawer, so no doubt there might have been a little something left in there of hers, and while Lily was alive indeed, the woman who took care of her had issues with her feet. Of course, the rodent's vision would be at foot level, so she'd connect with her good human friend over a detail involving feet. Interspecies communication and mediumship at its finest!

So in the Realm of Mind, the consciousness of the spirit of the person who crossed over, my consciousness, and the consciousness of the person I'm reading for all meet and try to communicate with each other through sensations, symbols, and commonalities. In the Realm of Form, the world you engage with your five senses, you communicate with words—at least, you can do that if you speak the same language as the people you're talking to. If not, what do you do? You speak with body language, including gestures and tone of voice, and you mime actions to get the point across. Nonverbal messages are more universal, but even then, you can accidentally misinterpret the message received. Now you can understand why Spirit communicates to you in the Realm of Mind using imagery.

MOVING INTO THE OTHER REALMS

Intuition is an inherent primary skill—our first sense, as I said—and a gift from the Realm of Spirit that we discover and use in the Realm of Mind to access insights, information, and energy the intellectual part of the mind can't perceive. With all that available to use, we can access our courage. Trust me, we need it if we're going to look at our own role in our stories without being crippled by shame, harsh judgment, and embarrassment. If we focus on *faults*, we can start to feel horrible about ourselves and shut down as the small self rushes in to distract us from the pain of self-examination. But if we focus on the roles we've played in our stories, being as objective and as compassionate as we can—ah, that's a different story.

This fearless inventory I'm describing takes place in the Realm of Light, which is the next in the sequence of interconnected realms. There, the dark corners of our psyche become illumined. What we stuffed here or there out of discomfort can no longer be denied. In the dark cupboard under the stairs lies the hidden, forgotten self—a powerful natural wizard who just needs love, encouragement, training, and some great companions to be able to practice extraordinary magic. (Yes, that's a Harry Potter reference!) What is in the shadows is neither good nor bad, although the form it has taken in the material world might be very ugly. You may have lied, or taken advantage of someone, or harmed yourself because you didn't recognize your power to create a new life for yourself.

It's okay. We all do it. I had a lot of skeletons in that closet that I had to bring to life and reintegrate into myself in a new form in order to become the person I am today. The light is a light of awareness and transformation. What you once feared or hated can become what you love and celebrate. Parts of yourself that you denied will continue to haunt you if you don't do the work of traveling to the Realm of Light and facing what you need to know about yourself.

Next in the sequence comes the Realm of Energy. Here you become aware that everything is energy, and energy is always in motion. That's true in the matrix of reality: Even a still pond has movement within it—creatures and molecules and atoms and undercurrents. Nothing stays the same, but if you can embrace the magic of movement, you can harness the force to bring your dreams into manifestation. Here is where you can direct the water, the wind, and even the flames of the fire emitted from the dragon's mouth so that instead of burning you, the force allows you to cook—or roast marshmallows! As always, it's important to do the work of transformation with lightness and joy. Sincerity and earnestness are marvelous, but you can get weighed down by the seriousness of the work you have to do in this life, and that can trigger the small self's fear. The more you laugh, the easier life is. Laughter makes the heart dance like a feather on the wind or a fallen leaf in the currents of a creek.

In the Realm of Energy, our intention forms because the possibilities begin to coalesce into will. We were inspired and now we want to move! We want to see our ideas manifest in the Realm of Form. With our intention, we direct the energy that flows. The power to create is here, and it allows us to become the wizard we were all along.

Finally in our sequence of interconnected realms, you get to the fifth one, the Realm of Form, where all that occurred in the other three realms unified within the Realm of Spirit is made manifest in the world of the senses. Here, you see the results of what you have co-created. Whom you meet, what you experience, and everything you achieve, acquire, touch, taste, and feel can take countless forms, but all of it will reflect what has been co-created in the energetic Realms of Spirit, Mind, Light, and Energy.

You'll learn more about how to work with these four realms in the chapters ahead, but always keep in mind that your tickets to ride this marvelous carnival attraction, otherwise known as a joyful and ever-evolving life of purpose and meaning, are gratitude and intuition. Thanks be to Spirit for these gifts. Let the fun begin!

And life *is* fun, even when in the Realm of Form, where it can become very challenging. I know that in my heart and in my bones. Follow the signs of intuition, keep talking to Spirit and saying, "Thank you! I trust you!" and "Please, show me a sign, I'm freaking out here!" because Spirit wants to reassure you. Pay attention, and remember that Spirit loves to play. You never know how those messages will show up and guide you. In the pages ahead, I'll tell you a story from my own life that will show you just what I mean.

SOME HAVE A YELLOW BRICK ROAD, I HAVE A DRAGONFLY

After my motorcycle accident, after I had realized I had to reclaim my gift of intuition and speaking with those on the other side of the veil, I began praying for communication from Spirit about where I was heading, literally. Where was I supposed to go? I had moved from Sedona, Arizona, to New Hampshire, and I felt I needed to be closer to New York City to support my career. But was that the right move for me or for Marc and our furry creatures? I know that when I ask, I will receive, which is one important aspect of creating a dialogue with Spirit. I never quite know how the communication will begin, what the timing will be, or which medium Spirit will use, which is why remaining curious, open, and unattached to the form the guidance will take is as important as trusting that the guidance will come.

When I'm seeking guidance, I often say my favorite prayer, which you can use too:

> Thank you for all the goodness in my life, for all the beauty and meaning. Thank you for showing me the next right action. Show me a sign of what I need to know in order to be in alignment with your will. Thy will be done through me.

I said that prayer over and over and summoned Spirit through a deep and abiding gratitude. All day long, I kept saying thank you. And I started to feel the magic of Spirit pulsing everywhere. *Abracadabra.* Thank you, the words of gratitude, opened the door.

Soon I began to be visited by a huge red dragonfly that would follow me everywhere as soon as I stepped out the door. It was beautiful, larger than any dragonfly I had ever seen before, and decidedly red in color when I typically noticed and was attracted to the ones that were blue or green. I couldn't help noticing it the first time it showed up, and later when it followed me to the grocery store and to the mailbox, hovered nearby when I sat outside with coffee on my deck, and buzzed around when I went to tend to my hydrangeas. While it's true that dragonflies are everywhere in nature and around where I lived at the time, I seemed to be the only one of my friends to have this specific relationship with one, which was three times the size of the rest. Maybe it wasn't always the same dragonfly, but why did it seem to be everywhere when I'd never seen one like it before?

Even Marc thought there was an odd consistency to a huge red dragonfly suddenly appearing wherever I went. I could feel and sense this was the way Spirit would carry out its messages to me. *Okay, Spirit, dragonfly it is!*

I had been avoiding my motorcycle since recovering from my accident because my anxiety about riding was still lingering. My rational mind told me that I should think about how dangerous motorcycles are and maybe let go of my love of riding them. But I could not let fear defeat me! Every time I went near a motorcycle, it was as if a giant fire-breathing dragon were coiled around it, waiting to turn me into charred meat. But I had to return to riding. If I was going to quit, it would be because I knew it wasn't for me, not because I was terrified and defeated. To my amazement, I found there was no dragonfly nearby on the days when I didn't feel safe enough within myself to get on my bike. I felt a low-grade anxiety, a sense of distraction and disconnectedness, on those days. Then on days when I got the courage to get back on to take even a short spin on my bike, I felt plugged into Spirit—and wouldn't you know, the red dragonfly would show up in my driveway as I got on the bike and on the other end when I got off!

I began to intuit a relationship between when I was spiritually aware, allowing my soul self to lead, and when I was in fear or contracted into my small self. When my soul was engaged and my awareness was clear, there the dragonfly would be. When I was worrying too much about the mundane world, her absence became a nudge to realign with the higher truth in spite of the temporary outer conditions that might have set me off.

I began to ask for a dragonfly to show me when I was on track and when I was off track. This became my own personal oracle in nature. And when it showed up when I wasn't looking for it, I paid even greater attention to what was in front of me. It was like Spirit was playing the dragonfly game with me! My faith that I was being looked after grew. I paid closer attention to my soul awareness too and practiced my thank you Abracadabras with increasing fervor. Of course, life began to fall into place again, I became a better rider, and in the end I recommitted to the sport. My soul self and small self were working well in tandem.

Noticing the red dragonfly's connection to me around my motorcycle helped me to gain insights into myself, my relationship to motorcycle riding, and my need to let go of my fears and stay in my lane rather than sticking to the safety of driving a car, giving logic more value than intuition. My motorcycle riding was a metaphor for trusting in Spirit and my relationship to my Higher Power.

But I did not close myself off to how the red dragonfly might lead me on back roads I didn't expect to be riding. I trusted in the will of Spirit, which led me to my new home and to helping a woman connect with the spirit of her brother—a very important connection Spirit wanted me to make for her.

It made sense to be closer to New York for my career, and that was in alignment with my soul's journey, I felt. I had a strong sense that Marc and I had to move to that area, and thankfully, my husband trusts my relationship to Spirit on these matters. Although the timing always seems to be strange, we know to just go with the sense that it is time to leave a home and relocate in a particular place. Marc agreed to move as long as he could be no more than an hour outside of New York City itself, and we went house hunting.

I'd just learned the Realtor I had been chatting with about finding a place near New York City had experienced a death in his family, so I was reassigned to another Realtor—a wonderful, warm, and accommodating woman who committed herself to help us find a rental. I called to make an appointment with the female Realtor, and as soon as I heard her voice on the phone I felt a "ding" of recognition. For whatever reason, she happened to mention that she too had a recent death in her family.

Hmmm . . . Spirit's plot thickens.

The Realtor did not pry at all when I skirted the issue of what exactly I do for a living, saying only "I write books," which I say to keep from scaring off people who are supposed to do business with me (and, hello, it's just awkward to announce, "Well, I talk to dead people, create working oracles, and counsel and coach the living"). Flash forward to days later: After seeing so many homes that were so-so and so not right for Marc and me, I needed to go to the restroom. So I sat down on the toilet and asked Spirit to send me a sign (and yes, Spirit is ever present, which means you're not alone in the bathroom, although it can be easier to relax and do your business if you don't think about that). I was not expecting a dragonfly in the bathroom. After all, I'd locked the door. But I was asking for whatever was supposed to happen since I was beginning to question my absolute trust in Spirit's taste in home rentals. And

I know Spirit is endlessly patient with us when our small self starts the Chicken Little routine and we pray, "Oh please, oh please, I know I should just relax and trust you but please, oh please . . ."

So there I was sitting down on the "throne," and all of a sudden I got the strongest sense of an electrician in overalls in the bathroom with me, telling me he wanted to talk to his sister. Um, spirit folks—timing and privacy, please?

So I acknowledged the spirit graciously before I finished up and flushed. Then, back in the car, wondering if I was completely off base and trying to swat the spirit away like one does with flies (because they are just as pesky as flies some of the time, I swear), I was finally overwhelmed with the need to tell our unsuspecting passenger about her brother. Hmmm . . . opening up a conversation like this is always a delicate one.

To make a long story short, here's how it went:

The electrician, with a lot of unresolved psychological issues when he was alive, came through in disjointed yet self-sorting puzzle pieces.

Me to Realtor: Hi. Was your brother an electrician? An addict—alcoholic?

Realtor (with eyes now open wide): Yes, he just passed away.

Me: In June. The 11th? [Yes, he really was that specific.] He says you need to remember talking about him by water? It's really important you remember that. Do you need to do something with this?

Realtor (with a look of shock on her face): Oh my God. My brother died on June 9 and was cremated on the 11th, and he specifically asked us to cast his ashes into the sea!

Me: You guys haven't released the ashes though, have you?

Realtor (eyes widening, voice shrinking): No.

Me: You guys need to release the ashes so you can release the guilt and cast it out to sea. He's at peace and happy.

Realtor: Oh my God. Yes, we all felt so guilty, especially my mom.

Me: He wants me to tell you, "I'm so not in hell!" Tell . . . Rose, nope, rose, roses, *rosary*? I see an old Catholic woman?

Realtor (in shock): Yes, my grandmother always said he was going to hell, and she says her rosary for him constantly.

And so it went all afternoon, and as more and more was revealed for her, I realized I'd been sent on this trip for the sake of this woman and her family and not for the sake of looking at houses. Yes, I needed to find a house, but Spirit had other plans today!

The day ended and it was time to say good-bye. "One last thing"—I said as we dropped our shocked and curious Realtor off at her office—"he shows me images of you crying over a bicycle he refused to help you build when you were little. He says he's sorry he did that, and how he wrecked it. He wants me to tell you verbatim, 'Now do you believe it's really me? Talk to Ma, tell her I said she was an awesome mother. She did not make me this way. You guys need to let go of the guilt!"

I didn't sleep all night, and the next day our Realtor revealed she had spoken to her Italian mother about it all. They had been consumed by guilt. She told me her mother cried her eyes out and was so relieved, and now they both knew it was okay to let the ashes go.

And the last message about the bicycle? It was indeed the icing on Spirit's cake, because when the Realtor relayed it to her mother, Mamma blurted out in her thick Italian accent, "*Son-na-ma beetch*, its-a-really him!"

The family had found peace, and I made a new forever friend.

When we met to see the last batch of homes that were not for us, she gave me a gift in a box. I opened it. It was beautiful notepaper, with a border featuring dragonflies . . .

GETTING THE MESSAGE

So the moral of this story is that you and I may plan what our day is going to be like, set our goals, and take actions toward reaching them, but Spirit has the real plan. And no matter what you think you want, you will participate in what is supposed to happen. When you invoke Spirit, your soul's Map will always lead you in the right direction, even if it appears to be a detour. For you, the detour may be a job that makes you kick yourself, wondering, "Why did I take that awful job, and why did my intuition tell me to say yes to it, only to have the company restructure and dump me six months later?" You may not find out until a year later, or five years later. But sometimes Spirit makes it clear right away why you took a detour. In this case, I found out quickly and marveled at Spirit's brilliant plan for using me to be of service.

But back to the mundane world. Marc and I still needed a house! We hurried to Toronto, where I immersed myself in shooting the TV show as planned. As I mentioned earlier, I also did more consecutive mediumship readings than I ever had in my life. The dragonfly notepaper reminded me that no matter what, the perfect situation was on its way. It definitely helped to have that message from Spirit and to laugh at how clever Spirit can be in finding ways to get the message through to you. A message on notecards! I love it!

But thinking about my house hunt, I did wonder if my time looking near New York was meant only to serve the need of Spirit to connect me with Gina the Realtor (now my good friend) so that I could connect her with her brother's spirit. Maybe it wasn't about the house after all?

Using the analytical mind to decipher signs is like trying to turn on a light with a blowtorch. You're not working with the right toolbox. I spoke to my feng shui adviser, the amazing Angel de Para at www.earthluck.org, about my sense that Marc and I needed to move. What was it about? Angel concurred that my beautiful house, which we loved so much, no longer was energetically in alignment with Marc and me and moving was exactly what we needed to do. Because he has always been uncannily accurate about the energy of my environment and what we could expect in certain places, I listened. Then I asked Spirit for a very specific scenario that included an east-facing house, which would support us energetically according to feng shui principles. I prayed, "Spirit, could you make it easy for this to happen if it be your will? Put up roadblocks if I have lost my mind and you have an entirely different idea of where we're supposed to go. I am fine either way. No attachment."

We returned to the States, put our house up for sale—and it sold in three days.

The second day of our house-hunting tour, I was overcome with a sense that Spirit was the one who would pick the house, not me. Marc and the dogs and I were now living in a hotel and too exhausted to go through a guessing game. So I asked for a dragonfly to show us the house we were supposed to buy.

We went from house to house like Goldilocks. Most weren't east facing, some were too big, some too dark, one too old and one definitely haunted, and many too expensive. One had a dead bird on it, while the others had stinkbugs but no dragonflies. I tried to convince myself that a bluish housefly was Spirit's substitute for a dragonfly near a house with a swimming pool (because I wanted a pool) before I realized I was just letting my frightened small self ignore my inner knowing that, no, this wasn't the house. As this went on, Marc and I both started second-guessing ourselves. What had we done?

Then a house suddenly came on the market, and we went to see it because even though it didn't fit our wants, it totally fit our needs. We arrived in a bad mood, but there was something about the Realtor who met us there. She was a beautiful woman with sparkling eyes and a huge white smile. I couldn't put my finger on why I felt so strongly about her. In conversation we found we had close mutual friends in common. I knew I was supposed to meet her.

At this point Marc was not having any of it. He didn't like the house, was tired of my signs and omens, was convinced Spirit had nothing to do with our Map, and gave me the "Can we leave now?" vibe as soon as we'd finished a brief tour. I lingered by the steps saying good-bye to the Realtor. Just then, far off in my peripheral vision, I saw what I thought to be a hummingbird, or maybe a toy helicopter. Lo and behold the biggest dragonfly I had ever set eyes on flew over and circled slowly around us.

This was my sign! Thank you, Spirit! It should have been a slam dunk right then and there, but Marc said no way. He was not having anything to do with my dragonfly sign.

The next day, we decided to revisit the house before going back to the hotel. I solicited the help of my parents in Spirit. They always had good house karma. I asked for another sign. I reminded Marc about how my mom shows up in ladybugs, and my dad shows up in monarch butterflies, and dragonflies and ravens come to me when Spirit wants me to pay attention. He nodded with a tired and stern look on his face.

I was torn and feeling unsupported by my number one cheerleader. My heart told me not to ignore the dragonfly, but I didn't want to be in conflict with Marc.

We went back to the house to look again, with Marc resigned and me hopeful. He was in another room when I heard him say, "Colette, you should come look at this."

I was worried he was going to show me a nest of termites or something. Instead, Marc, surrendered and smiling, pointed to a framed picture of a monarch butterfly—the symbol for my father. Convinced that we were not going to take the house, the Realtor had placed some new decorative touches around to help stage it. The photo had not been there the day before.

We got the message. We moved in two weeks later.

The lesson here is that Spirit delivers exactly what we need when we need it. Not always what we *want* but what we *need.* I got a dragonfly, and then a monarch butterfly—and a house, and a great new friend.

A TORCH IN THE DARK

These stories are specific to me and Marc, but their truth applies to you too. If you're willing to begin a conversation with Spirit, you automatically ignite your soul just like you're lighting a torch to see in the dark. Invoking the Realm of Spirit is magical because the most amazing, illogical things begin to happen, and all manner of meaningful coincidences line up to make sense of it all. The uncharted is revealed to you in perfect harmony as you travel from Mind to Light to Energy to Form.

I began in the Realm of Mind, connecting to Spirit—every day, throughout the day. I began receiving signs and intuiting what I needed to do. Then I traveled to the Realm of Light. I shed light on the part of myself that I have to claim and integrate, the intuitive self that helps people communicate with those who have crossed over, and brought it back into my awareness without shame. I allowed myself to look totally woo-woo when I offered to pass along messages to the two Realtors I was working with. I allowed myself to look foolish to my husband, who was finding that this time, the "follow your intuition" approach to house hunting made him doubt the ways of Spirit. I let Spirit use me even if it made me uncomfortable.

Regardless of the temporary flux of outer conditions, I had to keep faith in what was being illuminated for me as signs in my world. I had to trust that there was meaning and purpose in the most unusual and illogical things. I had to trust the outcome.

From the Realm of Light, I could move into the Realm of Energy. I took actions that aligned with what I had learned and experienced in the first two realms, and I continued saying no to houses that some would say were perfectly acceptable. I trusted Spirit and this process of co-creation. We would change where we were living, and it would work out, even if we were temporarily homeless and exhausting all the listings in the places where we were looking.

And what happened ultimately? We stayed in the house we'd found for eight months before another series of undeniable synchronistic events lined up, and lo and behold, in the Realm of Form was manifested the house we really needed but also had always wanted for this stage in our lives. This house is in Canada, in a place near where we have friends, far enough from Toronto that we can enjoy the natural world but close enough that I can get to wherever I need to go to do a personal appearance or have a business meeting. My mind would never have thought about going back to Canada or looking for a house like the one we found. The Mind of Spirit's plan was so much better than what I could cook up. Tapping into it and co-creating with it worked out far better than I could have imagined.

I manifested what I desired, and I also changed internally. I became someone better at integrating my intuitive gifts into my identity and into my everyday life. This journey through the realms was not as harrowing as the journey I took in the hospital bed, where I had to evolve in order to get back in the right lane with my career. But both journeys involved my doing the work of the five interconnected realms in order to emerge more authentic, more evolved, and better prepared for what I said I wanted to create for myself. There would be challenges to living near Toronto again (which I'll tell you more about in Chapter 10: "The Realm of Form"), and I knew I could face them now.

So are you ready to use the five interconnected realms to co-create what you desire *and* become the person you need to be in order to be comfortable with what you co-create? Next you'll learn more about working with your consciousness and that of Spirit in the Realm of Mind.

Traveler's Notes

- On the Map of the soul, there are five interconnected realms. The Realm of Spirit is a center hub that transcends, infuses, and unites four other realms—Mind, Light, Energy, and Form.
- The Realm of Spirit makes itself obvious to you once you learn to align with it, dialogue with it, and decipher its messages. Spirit will reveal itself through signs, synchronicities, messages, nature, and people.
- Our problem with co-creating what we want is that we start in the Realm of Form, the last of the realms, when we should be starting in the Realm of Spirit and doing the work of the other four realms, working our way around to the realm where manifestation happens.

- Wish well, from the Realm of Spirit, before trying to manifest what you think you want. It's important not to be too attached to the exact form it will take. Spirit might have a much better version for you. The essence is more important than the form.
- From the Realm of Spirit, you enter the Realm of Mind and begin to transform within. Remember that thoughts are powerful when you are co-creating. The right use of thinking is essential: As we think, so shall we be.
- Next you go to the Realm of Light and take a fearless inventory of what lies in the shadows of your awareness. What you once feared or hated can become what you love and celebrate, and what you thought could never be yours can turn out to have been yours all along.
- Next in the sequence comes the Realm of Energy, where you harness the force to bring your dreams into being as possibilities begin to coalesce into will.
- Finally you get to the fifth realm, the Realm of Form, where all that occurred in the other three realms unified within the Realm of Spirit is made manifest in the world of the senses.
- When you invoke Spirit, your soul's Map appears and you head in the right direction to have the experiences your soul desires.
- Listen to your intuition and know the limitations of your analytical mind. Using the analytical mind to decipher signs from Spirit is like trying to turn on a light with a blowtorch. You're not working with the right toolbox.

7

THE REALM OF MIND

The Realm of Mind is the first location on the Map of the soul that you visit after orienting yourself in the Realm of Spirit. It's where your consciousness intermingles with Spirit, the consciousness of the matrix of energy. In the matrix, everything—every event and experience—exists as pure potential. It's the primordial soup where form starts as an idea. Plato recognized that every concept has a pure form that can't exist in our world, only in our awareness. Human attempts to create something of pure beauty, or a system of perfect justice, will always fall short because of the limitations of the human mind. But we can always strive to take those perfect ideas that exist in the matrix and bring them into our lives here on earth. The work really begins after we've immersed ourselves in the Realm of Spirit and stepped onto the Map of the soul. Here's where your intentions should begin to take shape—not in the Realm of Form, where your thinking is dominated by your nearsighted and shortsighted small self.

This thing we call the mind is more complex and multilayered than we think it is. The wiser we become, the more we realize the potential of our minds. Wisdom breaks us free of the limitations of the mind and its thoughts and beliefs that are based in memories etched on the familiar Map. In fact, the mind is designed to be efficient and lead us back to familiar territory again and again. Our job is to stop being so efficient and automatic and instead immerse ourselves in the co-creative, evolutionary process that begins with the work of understanding the mind.

Being on autopilot—doing the same thing over and over again despite a conscious decision to do something differently—can be thought of as being trapped in a story. Stories are how we make sense of what has come before and how we predict what will come next. Our minds make it easy for us to do the same old same old and live according to a well-established narrative. Co-creating something new and better requires you to take ownership of the choices you've made that led to your story of what happened and how it happened. Radical acceptance, surrendering to the truth without judgment and without attachment to it, is the key.

Here's how to practice radical acceptance: You have to take ownership not just of your conscious choices but of the unconscious ones that led you to symbolic places within the Map of your psyche like the Storm Fields where you had to dodge lightning strikes or the Barren Desert where you believed nothing would ever grow and you'd wander forever without sustenance. It's natural to say, "I didn't know I was making a mistake—I couldn't help it." Listen, it's not fun to admit that while your story about yourself has been influenced by other people and things that just seemed to happen "to" you, it was also co-written by you personally to a large degree. Fate played a role, to be sure, but you can take much greater control over your "fate." As Carl Jung is supposed to have said, "Whatever is not brought from the unconscious into the awareness seemingly comes to us as fate." Awareness is the gift of the Realm of Mind.

The narrative you shaped—your story, as Jung called it—helps you to understand your experiences, so don't beat yourself up over it. Over time, your central story became so familiar that you identified with it and it served as a familiar Map that pulled you back to well-trodden territory over and over again. So here, in the Realm of Mind, you want to identify your story so you can stop identifying *with* it and free yourself from it! If you stick to your story, it will stick to you. You have to dis-identify with it to change it. That means recognizing it, which is the work in the Realm of the Mind, but it also means letting go of the shame and discomfort attached to your story—which you'll learn to do in the Realm of Light.

When I was changing my brand, I was changing my story. I consciously chose to leave out the bit about my being able to communicate with those who have passed. I tried to take a shortcut in the co-creative, evolutionary process. I jumped from the Realm of Mind straight to the Realm of Form; I skipped the part where I had to actually do the work of transformation and self-acceptance. I wanted to be something different to avoid pain and feeling shamed by other people, and I wanted it now, now, now! I didn't trust in the Map of the soul and I didn't accept how important this evolutionary process is.

I am an example of someone who knows all this intimately, and even teaches it, yet still I took a detour, still I refused the call, still I watched helplessly as nothing worked or fit me right, and still I tried to lead with the small self. I share my experience with you to give you something to relate to, and then to show you how I was able to move through it to the other side. Even with the detours, I was able to recalibrate and start engaging in right thinking (in the Realm of Mind), illuminate the shadows and shed light on the overlooked and brushed aside parts of myself (in the Realm of Light), and take action (in the Realm of Energy)—then surrender the results (allowing what I desired to manifest in the Realm of Form, thanks to the help of Spirit).

You, too, have parts of your story you'd just as soon leave out of a new story, I'm sure, but I can show you how to keep them and use them differently. That way, you'll be better prepared to find the courage to go to the uncharted places—and you will set yourself up to find magic there. Trust me, this process works, and Spirit's there by your side helping you with this co-creative evolution. You change, what you want gets stripped away to its essence, and what shows up in form is what you most want and need.

Now it's time to wrap your mind around your mind so you can understand how it creates stories and how you can write better ones.

THREE MINDS IN ONE

Sigmund Freud was the first to identify the ego, or what I call the small self or small mind. He explained that there are actually three minds or aspects of the mind: the ego, the subconscious, and the unconscious. The ego is your personality, while your subconscious is your memory that you can easily retrieve. Think of it like a file on your hard drive that you don't have open at the moment but that you can click open at any time. The unconscious is your deepest memory storage space—it's the part of your hard drive's memory where you keep everything you ever put in your computer, including your operating system. You don't think about it, although it's running all your programs. (By the way, I have to thank Mindset-Habits.com for that helpful computer metaphor.)

What if you could rid yourself of those old fears you inherited or that became instilled in your subconscious many years ago? You would need to become aware of your patterns embedded in your subconscious. It's the subconscious that is bringing up to your conscious small mind memories and patterns of thinking and feeling that were determined by past experiences. Your subconscious reminds you of the familiar. But it usually denies you access to the oldest memories, stored in the unconscious, that are affecting it. Unconscious memories may be carried over from previous lifetimes, or they may be memories of the soul's experience behind the veil, where it set intentions for what to experience in this life.

Your small mind filters out a lot of information to prevent you from going crazy trying to process it all. The subconscious takes in everything, holds on to some of it, and moves much of it to your mind's deep storage space—into the corners of the unconscious. While your small mind works with a limited amount of information at any given time, your subconscious functions as an efficient autopilot where you store all your biases. These are the preconceived ideas that help you make sense of your past and current experiences and plan for the future. It's your subconscious that holds on to prejudices and internalized beliefs about "someone like you" whom you should aspire to be. It's also your subconscious that remembers all your failures and will bring them up to you, wrapped in a blanket of anxiety, when you're faced with a challenge. Any subconscious pattern is an actual pathway in your brain, a neural network of brain cells and synapses that you can rely on to simplify your thinking and make you believe the old story. And what's key to remember is that when you have feelings about that old story, they are based in perspective and perception, not a "truth" fixed in time and space.

REPROGRAMMING YOUR SUBCONSCIOUS

To break free of the familiar patterns, you have to do three things. First, you have to commit to changing your conscious thoughts. Chances are you already work at thinking positively and optimistically, so I'm not going to go into that step in detail. Just know that changing your internal narrative really does matter, so be conscious of what you're saying to yourself all day long and correct it. (Affirmations can help with this.) Second, you have to let go of feeling foolish or embarrassed about ending up in the same old place thanks to your subconscious mind's autopilot. And third, you have to tell your subconscious mind to imagine something better. To take those second and third steps, you have to reprogram your subconscious mind, which is not smart like your conscious mind is. It's not wise either. It is your autopilot, effectively re-creating the old beliefs over and over.

Don't think I'm saying your subconscious brain's autopilot is a bad thing. It acts as a valuable filter. If it didn't, you'd be overwhelmed by all that your mind has to process. You'd be distracted by everything from that squirrel running up a tree, to every memory you ever had, to every little thing your senses pick up on. Your subconscious mind scans what's in front of you for any signs that you're unsafe—based on its programming. If it sees signs of danger, it goes into panic mode. If it doesn't see signs of danger, it tries to help you make sense of what you're experiencing by referring back to what you experienced in the past.

To switch off the autopilot and retrain the subconscious mind, you can pretend that you are experiencing something very different, using your imagination. Several studies have shown that basketball players who practiced free throws in their minds improved their actual free-throwing ability as much as players who stood on the basketball court aiming and throwing real basketballs into the net.

The players who used their imaginations actually formed a new "memory" and reprogrammed their subconscious minds.

You can also use visualization and imagination to reexperience a memory differently, envisioning a different outcome and expressing the emotions associated with it as if the new memory were real. Your subconscious doesn't know that what it's experiencing in the present as you use your imagination to create a new memory or revise an old one is *not* real. Practice, practice, practice, and you'll reprogram your subconscious mind.

Dr. Joe Dispenza wrote the book *Breaking the Habit of Being Yourself,* and it's full of guidance on how to rehearse your new self or "fake it till you make it." As he wrote, "When you begin to feel like some potential future reality is happening to you in the moment that you are focusing on it, you are rewriting your automatic habits, attitudes, and other unwanted subconscious programs." You instill a new "memory" that your subconscious thinks is real, and these memories add up to a new story of who you are and how you will be as you sail into uncharted waters.

Creating something new, experiencing something very different from what's familiar, requires you to turn off the autopilot and stop being reactive so you can respond with detached awareness. It requires you to have new experiences, even if they're just in your imagination at first. What a gift imagination is! I created the Invision Process (now called the Total Mindshift Process) to provide an immediate shift in perspective to help us access something Carl Jung called *active imagination* as a catalyst for transformation. The ability to co-create a new story for ourselves is our superpower. Linking our imagination with the deepest layers of the personal mind—the *unconscious*, the collective unconscious, and the soul self—is the purpose of the Total Mindshift Process. (In this book I'm introducing you to the rudiments of the process, but if you're interested in learning more, I offer beginner and advanced courses on my website, and Hay House also offers my popular class Reprogram Your Subconscious Mind.)

You don't have to settle for a slightly improved variation on the old story—you truly can make big changes in your life and have them stick. In the uncharted places, total reinvention and inspired co-creation are possible. Working with Spirit, you are the ultimate innovator in the art of storytelling. Inspiration, the deepest creativity, comes from the soul, which is guided by Spirit. In fact, the word *inspiration* comes from a root that means "to breathe into," suggesting the breath of Spirit entering into us.

This deep, creative work of personal evolution can't happen if you're not mindful of how you work your mind and its layers of consciousness. When you remain mindful, you notice that you're operating from your old programming. This makes it easier to commit to entering the uncharted areas and make a new choice to open to inspiration and new experiences.

Sometimes we are challenged to evolve very quickly, and it's tempting to skip the steps of co-creative evolution. In fact, I'd say all of us on the planet are facing this challenge right now. We're straining the earth's resources, and we have to write a new story of collaboration, conservation, and sustainability. At the same time, social media and mobile devices have so dramatically changed our experiences that any of us can instantly find ourselves in the middle of an emotionally powerful experience simply because we were scrolling through a social media site out of boredom. We have to evolve our brains and minds to be able to handle the emotional challenge of constant stimulation and the stress that comes with it. We're called to meet the challenge of resisting the same old responses and experiencing a new self in real time. We need Spirit as our co-creator more than ever before!

WORKING WITH THE GREAT MIND TO CO-CREATE

I'm convinced what we're experiencing is a new stage in human evolution. We're moving into the field of epigenetics—altering the way our genes express themselves. As we begin to reprogram our subconscious, the unconscious mind starts to be affected, because ego, subconscious, and unconscious are all interconnected. And the unconscious is a part of something even larger than ourselves: the Great Mind, where every memory and possibility exist. Tap into the

Great Mind and the potential for change is extraordinary. You access your magical powers to co-create something completely different from what you've known before.

Your unconscious mind is the portal to the Great Mind and links directly with your soul self. While the small mind might be able to intellectually understand the Great Mind, it does so by trying to define it, as if the Great Mind were separate from our minds and us. The small mind always perceives separation, but we are never separated from the Great Mind. The unconscious, on the other hand, is able to perceive the connectedness and unity of all that exists. It is aware of the Great Mind encompassing and unifying all consciousness. The matrix is neutral and impersonal because it has everything, both positive and negative, both shadow and light, within it, but the Great Mind, or Spirit, is pure love.

In my book *Remembering the Future,* I described an extraordinary experience I had when I was in a meditative state. I was scooped up by what I came to understand was an angel, who whisked me away to a place where other angels were playing. They tossed me around like a beach ball before returning my consciousness to my body. I'll never forget marveling at the net of light that made up the angels' wings, realizing that what people over the ages have thought of as white feathers are actually filaments of light and tangible nets of energy that make up the wings. I remember understanding that the human mind tries to comprehend these extraordinary visions and experiences by relating them to experiences we have in the world of our senses. We couldn't understand the world beyond the senses if we didn't do this.

The Great Mind has been described in many ways, but people's perception of it is limited by their personal experiences and the limitations of language. I now understand that whether we're talking about many gods, like in polytheistic religions (Hinduism, for example), or one God, like in monotheistic religions (Judaism, Christianity, and Islam being the most common ones), we're talking about the same thing. Some have perceived the many and others have perceived the one. People have gone to war over differences in their belief systems and argued, "We're the real Christians and those people are not" because of what they believe about the Trinity (Father, Son, Holy Ghost, as I was taught in Catholic catechism). Three gods, or three faces of God? Many gods or one?

The answer is all of the above. I understood that intellectually a long time ago, but I've been reminded of it directly through my experience of listening to Fred. Our little minds just can't comprehend the Great Mind, but that's okay. As long as we know how to open the doors of perception (as first William Blake and then Aldous Huxley described it) or the portal of connection known as the unconscious mind (as Carl Jung described), we can awaken from the spiritual narcolepsy we agreed to experience in human form and remember the nature of Spirit. Yes, we're of Spirit and in Spirit, connected to Spirit, and an expression of Spirit. It's easier to understand this when you experience it than when you read words on the page, believe me. But it's what the great religious writings have tried to described—"I am the alpha and the omega," "I AM," "The Tao is all things." Spirit is unity yet with many facets, like a jewel or prism.

Your soul's consciousness is connected to your small mind as well as to the Great Mind in the same way that a cell membrane, which we think of as a separate, physical structure, is actually a conduit that moves information and nutrients between the cell and the environment. For many years, scientists believed the cell membrane was simply a wall that had the job of holding all the stuff inside a cell together. But as biologist Bruce Lipton has pointed out in his books, such as *The Biology of Belief*, when it comes to cells, the membrane is the true brain of the cellular operation. Our consciousness works the same way. It's actually the "brains" of the organization, shaping our bodies while communicating with all of creation and the matrix of life that includes the Great Mind. The newest findings in consciousness research imply that the brain is like a radio receiver for the mind, which surrounds the body and isn't actually generated by the brain. Your "brains" are not in your brain!

This is important to know, because it has everything to do with our breaking out of our old habits and bravely venturing forth into the uncharted. Our minds are vehicles and portals, not contained by our personal experiences and our bodies. Consequently, there are endless possibilities for finding new opportunities, new roads, new insights, and new energies that can give us the momentum we need to not just make changes but keep them going. When we know this and work with our consciousness, we open ourselves up to the magic in the uncharted places. But that means saying to the small mind, "Nice try, but let's open up and see what the Great Mind has to communicate." It means allowing the porous boundary of your consciousness to let in new information—and energy—from outside of your individual, small mind.

When I'm connecting with the other side, this porous boundary of my soul's consciousness acts as my portal, but when I need to turn it off and shut it down, I get grounded and focus on my physicality and go purposely into my small mind. I'm still aware of my connection, but I tune out much like turning off a switch. It's no different from turning off a radio. It doesn't mean the energies have disappeared. I'm just not listening anymore.

Consider the music that you stream through the radio or online. Where does this music go after you turn off the device you're listening to? It's still there in the energy waves that exist in the invisible spaces you and I can't sense with our five senses. The mind is capable of reaching far beyond the personal self, and it is always there, like radio waves. Once you turn off the radio, you don't stare at it wondering where the song you just heard is. You don't stare at it and contemplate what other music there might be floating around in the air. We're conditioned to automatically listen to music but not to concern ourselves with where it's coming from. Yet if you do, you'll get the picture of how the Great Mind works through yours.

Exercise: Imagining Your Connection to the Great Mind

Think of a talented musical artist you admire and imagine this person is sitting on a bench in meditation, feeling emotions about a life experience of hers (or his). This artist is thinking, and pondering words that could express this personal experience.

Now imagine this artist is tuning in to the experience, which is in the form of energy. The energy is swirling around her, and you can observe that her mind is tuning in to the symbolic aspects and translating it into sound.

But beyond the personal energy field you will notice a greater field, one you might imagine as being wider and farther reaching, that moves through and into the energy closest to the musician. This is a universal field she shares with others.

Now the artist is inspired (filled with Spirit) and energized to take action to co-create the music that spills out of her and into her instrument and voice. The personal becomes universal, and the soul that knows no separation shares this with others.

Now this song ends up at a radio station that will beam it out into the energy field.

You turn on the radio. The song is playing. You listen with your hearing and feel with your heart. You become one with the invisible artist, the invisible inspiration, the unified self, the impersonal self, and the Great Mind. As the notes tug at your heartstrings, you feel the resonance of the words, and you are changed as a result: you too are inspired.

Just imagine that you're able to see the energy of the Great Mind as waves of light that flow around and through the artist, and through the invisible world, and into you and every person who is inspired by it.

Now ask yourself this: *If the delivery system (radio) stopped functioning altogether, would that change anything in this scene?*

Would the life experience of the artist change?

Would the inspiration disappear?

Would the song still be written?

Would its existence cease?

If you think hard about this, you'll realize that the radio being on or off doesn't change the frequency of what's been co-created, nor the actual existence of the song. The song exists somewhere whether you're listening to it or not.

As I think about where the songs go when you turn off the radio, I understand that this is what Fred meant by repeating, *"We are We; You are We; We are When You Listen."* Fred is a consciousness collective that disappears entirely from my personal sphere of experience until I choose to turn on my awareness, much like turning on the radio.

The question we all need to ask ourselves is, what do we listen to? Can we choose our thoughts? Thoughts initiate reality. We look for evidence that our thoughts are correct—this is called confirmation bias (*Hey! Look! I was right!*). We look for mirrors. So if you don't feel safe, you look out into the world and find the reflection of your feeling of insecurity, and then your insecurity grows along with your story about why you're justified in feeling scared and unsafe. These belief systems get into our cells and affect our gene expression. There's a famous saying "As a man thinketh in his heart, so is he," and this captures this idea of how our thoughts and feelings become physical reality. They are that powerful.

Thanks again, Fred.

Excellent.

WHEN THE SMALL MIND TUNES OUT

Despite the unity between your small mind and the Great Mind, your small mind draws a big, dark curtain between itself and Great Mind when you give in to the string of negative chatter your small mind creates. All that noise and activity has it convinced that it is doing an important job in protecting you. Remember those dragons you need to train? They feed off the negative chatter about how you don't belong, how you're inadequate, and how everyone really just thinks you're an arrogant fool. They don't know the junk food you're feeding them is bad for them, but their growth will be stunted and their wings weak when you tell yourself, *See? I did it again. Stupid me!*

Your small mind notices your self-defeating inner narrative, remembers what you learned in that workshop or book about how bad it is for you, and goes right to judgment, creating thoughts like

I'm such an idiot! Look at me! "Yum, yum!" say the dragons like kids scarfing down candy loaded with sugar and chemicals. You have to learn to control that reaction, because it is actually reinforcing the old patterns—putting you right back on familiar roads without any nourishment for either you or your dragons.

One way to stop the chatter is through meditation. You have to get your small mind to pipe down, stop feeding the dragons garbage, and let that heavy dark curtain become translucent so you can access the Great Mind that is all consciousness.

I'm going to guess that many of you have tried meditation but aren't doing it regularly as a practice, because the small mind has convinced you that you're doing it wrong so you should just stop trying. "Yum, yum!" say the dragons. Ignore your small mind. Listen to me. You can do this. The very act of trying to pull your awareness back to the present moment, to your body and the energy that animates it, is meditation. If you can hold on to your awareness of your body and your breathing for more than a few seconds before your small mind starts pestering you again, that's fantastic. But if you can't, keep trying, because the trying is the work—the trying is the work. The more you practice, the easier it will get for you.

One of my friends regularly practices mindfulness meditation specifically and when she does it may be for just 10 or 20 minutes, but the work of practicing mindfulness when she's not sitting and focusing on her breath has paid off. She's able to thin that curtain into a translucent veil very quickly after sitting down to focus on her breathing, and she's aware of her monkey-like small mind's limited perceptions and beliefs as they come up for her. Everyone's different, and you may take longer to get to the point where you can do this easily, but research on meditation shows that you actually rewire your brain for greater self-awareness and reduced reactivity (in layman's terms, less intense freak-outs that happen less often) very quickly. In fact, groundbreaking research at Harvard using MRIs showed that beginner meditators using mindfulness meditation *changed their brains* in a matter of 27 minutes a day (on average) of meditation practice over eight weeks. That's just over 25 hours altogether.

I do sitting meditation for 45 minutes once a day, every day. I always start with the Total Mindshift Process to awaken my ability to observe what I'm experiencing while I am sitting and breathing. Then I do a walking meditation for 20 minutes daily, and if I have time, I do another 30 to 45 minutes later in the day. It not only thins that heavy, dark curtain but also makes it easier for me to tune in to my intuition, to communicate and dialogue with the Chorus Known as Fred, and to be self-aware in my everyday life. I can't imagine not doing it. When I meditate, I use variations of the same techniques. I love to play binaural beat music, which entrains the brain to produce brain waves associated with a trancelike state (alpha waves and theta waves). This is not the state of mind a person is in when the small mind is jumping around like a monkey—that involves different brain waves (specifically, beta waves).

Mindfulness simply means paying attention to your mind, noticing or observing its workings without judgment or shame or embarrassment that shut down your Observing Self. Your Observing Self is impersonal, and it is your authentic self or soul, that membrane-like structure made of energy and aware of your small mind and the Great Mind and itself all at once. It is the portal through which you can actually dialogue with Spirit.

Exercise: Observing the River of the Mind

Set a timer for 15 minutes to do this exercise. Find a spot to sit comfortably in an upright position with your back straight and both feet on the ground, shoulder-width apart, or sit in the yoga position if that is most comfortable.

Close your eyes and breathe deeply in and out six times. Just allow your body to relax with each inhalation and exhalation, paying attention only to your physical body. If there is any discomfort in your body, send a golden light into the areas where you feel tightness or pain, imagining that the light releases the tension and sends warmth and soothing energy to those spots. Then move on, allowing your awareness to scan your body, toes to head, for any other spots you may have missed that need healing light brought to them through the power of your awareness.

Now imagine a river in front of you, appearing as if your seat of awareness moved with you there. The water is flowing from left to right.

Imagine every thought you have now, no matter what it is, appears as a large leaf floating on the top of the water, moving to the right, each leaf disappearing down the river with the current, one after the other.

Let go the need to assign meaning to any of these thoughts that appear as leaves. Imagine they just come and go, floating by, and watch them with interest but detachment. They are just thoughts, just words, just memories, just images, just feelings, just leaves. They are all just leaves moving along a river.

Imagine that all of this is flowing out of you, out from around you into this river—just water and leaves pouring into the river. You are emptying your mind. Once there are no more leaves and the river's current begins to slow down, imagine the water begins to shimmer with light. It is the light of pure potential. The river is calm, natural, flowing. You're just watching it all.

When the timer goes off, come back to everyday awareness and write in your journal about your experience.

DIALOGUING WITH THE GREAT MIND OF SPIRIT

You can both receive messages from Spirit and dialogue with Spirit—yes, it is two-way communication! Ask for insights, answers to your questions, and reassurance.

My abracadabra for opening the door and starting the dialogue is gratitude. Feel the magnificence in the world and be thankful for it. That's how you get yourself to stop endlessly thirsting for what you don't have and creating a vibration of lack and scarcity. Gratitude removes ambition and clears space for a bigger dream than you would otherwise dream.

You can also start the dialogue by meditating on compassion, love, or peace. By "meditating on," I mean generating those feelings by focusing on these concepts. I don't mean write a wordy essay in your brain that your old English teacher would love. Words get in the way in dialoguing with Spirit and connecting with the Great Mind. Let images, sensations, and emotions arise as you meditate on these concepts.

You can open a dialogue using prayer or oracles. Earlier, I told you the story of my dialoguing with Spirit and receiving dragonflies as signs—while my husband, Marc, was seeing signs that we associate with my parents. We both had to interpret those symbols without having our small minds get in the way. It's the first sense, intuition, that dialogues best with Spirit, so it's important not to overthink what a message could mean. Let your heart and intuition guide you.

So now that you know your small self has a small mind integrated into your soul self's mind, integrated into the Great Mind, you can understand this: We are one mind. That's what the Chorus Known as Fred keeps reinforcing when I connect. *"We are We; You are We."* The unity consciousness has patches of awareness that are individual minds, just like a map has main roads, small roads, and even private driveways. They have similar qualities, but there's a big difference between someone's driveway and the interstate. There's a difference between what has been built on the surface of the terrain and what connects all terrains, all landscapes, below the surface.

Just as any driver can access your driveway and do a turnaround (whether it's legal or not!), anyone who taps into the Great Mind can, in the Akashic plane or matrix, tap into an individual mind. And there, in the matrix, lies all possibility. All roads run within the matrix. All roads lead to the Realm of Spirit, where you know this co-creative, evolutionary process is what you are supposed to engage in while you are here in form.

We all forget this is the truth when we come into our bodies. We think it's all about making our way in the world of form—competing, succeeding, and acquiring, finding acceptance and running away from pain. Our reluctance to start in the Realm of Spirit and work with the process of co-creative evolution locks us into our limiting stories. To make up for our loss of freedom, we convince ourselves that our stories give us security. As Byron Katie says, who are we without our stories? Yes, who are we, and who might we become?

What if the self you discover on your heroine's journey is a self far bigger than you imagined, a self with broader horizons and possibilities than you ever imagined? What if you could co-create a reality much more satisfying and meaningful than the one you feel confined in right now?

You can do that. Let's move further toward that goal and step into the next place on the Map of the soul: the Realm of Light.

Traveler's Notes

- The Realm of Mind is the meeting point of your consciousness and Spirit's consciousness, where you form intentions that are guided by Spirit and your soul, not your small self.
- The mind is designed to be efficient and lead you back to familiar territory again and again. You have to get beyond the limits of the small self's thinking.
- Awareness is the gift of the Realm of Mind. Take ownership not just of your conscious choices but of the unconscious ones you make.
- Your small mind filters out a lot of information. The subconscious takes in everything, holds on to some of it, and moves much of it to your mind's deep storage space.
- To break free of the familiar patterns, commit to changing your thoughts, let go of your fears of messing up, and reprogram your subconscious mind, which is not smart like your conscious mind is. It's an efficient autopilot doing what is predictable.

- Your subconscious doesn't know that what it's experiencing in the present as you use your imagination to create a new memory or revise an old one is not real.
- Identify your story so you can stop identifying with it and free yourself from it! If you stick to your story, it will stick to you.
- The ability to co-create a new story for yourself is your superpower.
- Linking your imagination with the deepest layers of the personal mind—the unconscious, the collective unconscious, and the soul self—is the purpose of the Total Mindshift Process.
- Ego, subconscious, and unconscious are all interconnected and a part of the Great Mind, where every memory and possibility exist.
- Your small mind draws a big, dark curtain between itself and the Great Mind when you give in to the string of negative chatter it creates and you forget to meditate and become quiet.
- Your soul is like a membrane made of energy, a portal through which you can actually dialogue with Spirit and be a conduit between your small self and the Great Mind.
- The Great Mind has patches of awareness that are individual minds, just like a map has many roads. All roads lead to the Realm of Spirit.

8

THE REALM OF LIGHT

The Realm of Light is where you connect with the light energy of Spirit, who knows and sees all. Spirit knows what is in the dark corners of your awareness—what Carl Jung called the shadow—and loves every part of you.

To participate in the joyful co-creation of a new life for yourself, you have to be an adventurer and explore this area of your mind: the subconscious. Here can be found treasures as well as moldy old junk you really need to bring light to so you can clear it out or clean it up. When you think of the cobweb-covered places in an attic or basement, you know the light of that 60-watt bulb isn't enough to help you see what's there. When you step into the Realm of Light, you gain the power of brilliant spotlights to show you what's been hidden from your conscious mind in the subconscious mind, which has no self-awareness. It simply does its job storing and retrieving memories.

In the Realm of Light, you can consciously choose what to reclaim and what to discard; you can decide what can be repurposed and how. And you can reprogram the subconscious so that it stores memories differently and attaches new emotional energy to them.

The task in the Realm of Light is to practice radical acceptance and forgiveness of yourself and others. This is the place of freedom and creativity, where Spirit and the mind commingle and create the spark that is the light of illumination, understanding, and transformation. The Realm of Light is like purifying fire that transforms the quality of painful memories so they no longer are toxic to you. The pain, sadness, and anger can be burned away, turning to smoke that dissipates or ashes that scatter to the wind.

Because light shining upon an object always casts a shadow, in the Realm of Light you have to face some darkness. But don't be afraid of exploring the hidden spaces that lie beneath the surface of your conscious mind. After all, you have Spirit at your side to help you tolerate the discomfort of the memories you access and the emotions you feel as you do this radical, honest exploration of yourself. On the Map of the soul, it's all good—but in the uncharted places where magic and creativity happen, you do have to meet and free the dragons that may be trapped there in the dark (or just not discovered yet in the unknown territories) in order to train them and restore their true purpose and power. Remember, you're not *slaying* the dragons. Dragons are not the enemy, even though they're wild creatures of power and fire. They're the source of *your* personal power, and if you get hurt when trying to interact with them, it's because you're supposed to change your relationship to your personal power. When you're working with dragons, you are not *destroying* your fear or its source. You're bringing the healing, transformative energy of light to it so your memories can live within you differently and the places that were wounded can be healed. Your personal power is balanced, and now you have access to a powerful ally to help you explore the places that exist outside the borders of your known universe. The dragons don't have to breathe fire on you because you know how to communicate and work with them.

This is the work that allows you to see the glowing silver paths on the Map of your soul—the lines connecting seemingly unrelated emotional experiences that used to leave you scratching your head. It all makes so much more sense when you look at the past with the Map of the soul. The shadowy spots and the dragons' lairs don't have to be quite so frightening after all.

Everything in the shadow, as Jung called it, has positive and negative aspects. Jung taught that it's helpful to think of the energies found in the shadow as archetypes. He identified some of them: the trickster, the warrior, the hero, the wise old man or woman, and so on. Others have suggested archetypes such as the scholar or the innocent. Archetypes are simply a way to understand the qualities of the energies.

Archetypes often take form as symbols, or when they reveal themselves to you during meditation, or when you're dreaming at night. The trickster within you could look like a fox, a jester, your favorite comedian, or you yourself when you are pulling a prank on your friends. Remember, Fred sent me an image that I later realized was the character Garth from *Wayne's World* to help me understand Fred's nature. Innocent, untainted, defender of the garden—that's Garth, and that's an archetype. Whatever you encounter in the dark spaces of your awareness, however it appears to you, even if it's unsettling—for instance, if you have a nightmare—don't be scared. It's simply energy that your mind is trying to make sense of through symbols and images.

So instead of having an old dresser drawer or box of photos in your mind's shadow storage, like you would have in an attic, what you have are archetypal energies wrapped around memories—and these memories and energies influence your everyday life in different ways. Your small self may have wrapped that energy in a blanket of fear or shame to protect you. But what if you could unwrap it and use its positive aspects to co-create something wonderful? I believe you need to do that to follow the call of your creative soul that is itching to have experiences it came here to have.

Although you may never have thought about what's hidden in the shadows of your awareness, and you may be afraid to explore it, none of these energies ever completely remains in the shadows anyway. They surface, and they affect what you attract and are attracted to, and your conscious mind has difficulty controlling the subconscious programming. Often, the small mind's awareness is so limited it has no idea what's hidden there in the shadow! But if you become aware of the shadow, you can work with its contents more effectively and even replace them with something better. That's the challenge of the Realm of Light, where the light is tangible Spirit, which affects energy or action, which in turn coalesces into form.

THE REBEL WITHIN

The Rebel is an archetype that lives within me and that you may recognize within you. Isn't there a part of you that wants to break free from the confines of your life and release all the beliefs and emotions and obligations that weigh you down? Is there a part of you that longs to hit the road while riding a powerful vehicle that can help you explore who you are and what you might become? That's how I feel on my Harley-Davidson motorcycle. The endless road of possibility stretches before me. I feel the wind and the sun enveloping me in their arms, and I know I'm at one with creation, supported by Spirit and the earth in all her splendor. I'm like the lilies of the field who neither toil nor spin, but are arrayed in beauty and always have everything they need thanks to Spirit. I can be wild and free and fully myself when I'm in touch with my wild nature. I connect in a positive way to the rebellious outsider I couldn't be when I was growing up.

The Rebel was my version of the Outsider, the archetype that haunted my mother and got passed down to me wrapped in fear and shame. The Outsider had always lived within me, but because of that fear and shame, she was hidden from my conscious awareness. Then the wild Rebel woman called out to me: "Colette, let me out! Free me!" She is what drew me to the "crazy" dream of becoming a singer/songwriter. She led me to explore the parts of myself that didn't fit in with everyone around me, that helped me meet people who were highly creative and who challenged me to be creative too. I am grateful to her for that. I'm glad I felt compelled to embody and express these aspects of the archetype. But oh, she had a dark side too, which caused me to drink too much and try drugs and eventually spiral downward into a full-blown addiction.

Because I feared my own power, I did not take ownership of my free-spirited, independent self. The energy was out of my control. I didn't know how to be a rebellious outsider in a way that served me. I didn't know how to allow my uniqueness to be okay. I didn't learn to ride the motorcycles I admired. Instead, I became involved with men who were outlaws and rode on the backs of *their* bikes—and followed them into an increasingly dangerous lifestyle. I so longed to experience and express my wild-woman outsider nature that I ignored the warnings about a biker bar I wanted to go to one day. I told my friends I could handle the danger—but I couldn't. Three men I knew offered me a lift home at the end of the night, long past the point when I knew I should have left. I didn't make it home. In fact, the events of that fateful night changed my life forever, as "home" was stripped away from me along with my self-worth and sanity.

Afterward, the archetypal Rebel crawled deep into the shadows and remained there for many years, hidden underneath my memory of terror. I came to associate motorcycles with the loss of my personal power and dignity.

Thirty-five years later, I had done much personal transformation work to heal the parts of myself that had been damaged. I had evolved, and I had reclaimed much of what had been hidden in the shadows. And as I was in the process of moving into a new home, I spotted just a few blocks away a huge Harley-Davidson dealership. Every day, I drove by it and felt a pull to stop in. It was as if my beautiful dragon I had claimed as my own wanted to stretch her wings wider than ever, nudging me to the edge of the past and into the uncharted future once more. There was still something haunting about being around motorcycles, and I wanted to challenge myself. Could I reclaim the wild Rebel woman within me and heal the old wound?

I am not the most graceful nor the most coordinated woman on the planet, so when I decided to get my motorcycle license at the tender age of 52, it was probably the most frightening thing I could ever do. Who would I become as a result of letting go of the old story of being a victim of the wild biker culture of my youth and all that happened to me back when I was at the wrong place at the wrong time? Could I become independent of that story and empowered by it instead? Could I come to tell a different story about that incident that for years toppled my choices like dominoes? I had already begun the process. The rape led me to claim my intuitive gifts and begin a new, more compassionate and honest relationship with my mother. I told the story countless times to help other women heal.

However, there was more rewriting of the story to be done—more healing that needed to happen.

It was a profound challenge to face my fear and the identity I'd built around those memories. I no longer wanted to associate motorcycles with my personal power being taken away from me. Besides, not all bikers are like those men! I no longer wanted my strong, wild, expressive female nature to lie buried within me, hidden under layers of fear and shame. I wanted to change the story and have the wild woman Rebel live differently in me.

I bought a bike that was huge and reflected the enormous amount of power I wanted to have, but the first day I rode it, I lost control. I dropped the bike when I couldn't turn on a corner and ended up with a split lip. Bleeding, I went back to Harley and bought their smallest one and started again (if you fall off the horse . . .). My husband watched me with pride and amazement as I kept getting up, and even after that serious accident when I ended up in bed for the summer, as I shared with you earlier, I still held on to my commitment to ride again. When I had recovered, I took my power back and rode a secondhand bike until I got all my courage back and more.

I made the commitment to overcome the fear, telling myself that if I were going to quit, it would be on my terms. I would not do it out of fear! With Spirit as my guide, I reclaimed my wild Rebel, fell in love with riding again, and ride often now with a greater respect for both the road and my own authenticity.

Today it's not the fact that I ride a motorcycle that empowers me. It's the fact that I created a new story of empowerment by releasing the past and building a new present. I choose to be fearless and worthy instead of remaining in the old story of a wounded young woman who lost her power to choose what happened to her and defined herself as dirty, unlovable, and broken. Riding for me is about retrieving the lost and abandoned parts of me on behalf of that confused, angry girl, restoring her dignity and power to write a new story—and to work differently with what was hidden in the shadows, bringing love and insight to heal the broken places.

THE LIGHT AND THE SHADOW CANNOT BE SEPARATED

In the Realm of Light, we recognize that light always exists in duality with a shadow—there's no avoiding it. There is always a dark side to everything, a contrast between what is nourishing and loving and what is draining and entangled in fear, anger, or hatred. Those emotions will always exist, but they don't have to overwhelm you or scare you away from the process of co-creation and transformation.

You have to accept that sometimes you will cry, get ticked off, lose something valuable, become preoccupied, and act selfish or insensitive—no amount of tapping, affirming, or meditating will give you the power to be perfect in every way. Trying your best is enough. It's all you can do. Knowing that makes it much easier to accept the shadowy parts of yourself and explore them to see how you might work with them differently. Love yourself—stay connected to the loving, accepting Higher Power that is Spirit—and this work will be much easier.

And what can you do with the parts of yourself you see as ugly and shameful? In the Realm of Light, you can see more clearly and observe that your initial judgment of them isn't necessarily accurate. For instance, if you look at selfishness, there are times when it's not a bad thing. Sometimes it's best for everyone if you attend to yourself and your needs first. It helps you reenergize and replenish yourself so that you don't get burned out and start operating from a primitive state of fear, anger, and desperation. It also allows you to set boundaries and teach others to recognize that everyone has limits and they need to look at their role in any situation or dynamic. Maybe they need to learn not to take so much or expect so much of you. Maybe your saying no will provide the impetus for them to overcome their own fears, enter the Realm of Light, and discover their power to do it themselves without you helping them or rescuing them.

The following exercise can help you discover and reintegrate parts of yourself that need to come out from the shadows of your awareness into the light.

Exercise: Mulch for the Garden, Art for the Soul

For this exercise, you'll need a journal, some basic drawing or painting or sculpting supplies, and some meditation music. You can do this on your own or with a friend. This exercise is in two parts. The first part is symbolic of how we can use the pain of the past as fertilizer for the future. The second part uses the process of creating art to express something beautiful from something ugly that you found through the exploration in the first part. If your small self is yammering on about how you aren't a real artist and you have no business picking up a piece of modeling clay to work with, tell it thank you for its concern but you are going ahead with this exercise to see what you can discover about yourself and your power to co-create!

You will need one full hour for this exercise.

First, choose your favorite meditation music that is soothing and calm, and set your timer for 15 minutes, which is the time you'll need for part one of this exercise—the part that uses the Total Mindshift Process.

Imagine you're soaring on the back of a beautiful dragon high in the sky. It's a beautiful day, and you are relaxed and secure on the dragon's back.

Imagine that you fly down to the ground and now find yourself in front of a building that represents the place where all your memories are stored.

Allow your mind to show the place to you rather than trying to create it through your directed imagination. Don't try to choose what the place will be or look like—your unconscious will provide the right image. Just allow it to be what it is even if it's an image that is unexpected.

Now you'll be drawn to either the attic or the basement. You're there to discover things from your past that have been hidden, broken, discarded, or left behind—things that you can use again in a different form. The objects will have stories that chatter away like music boxes or faraway voices; they echo the experiences that no longer serve you yet remain energetically within you, taking up space but without purpose.

Gather up these objects, or whatever you find, and join your dragon in the backyard.

You will see a beautiful garden. It is your Field of Dreams, where you've planted your intentions for a better today and a fruitful tomorrow.

Place what you found in a pile on the ground, and notice the things in it that may be decayed or dying. Remove them from the pile until all you have left are the objects that still seem interesting or useful or that call to you. Imagine you place those to the side.

Now bless all the objects with love and thank them for their service to you. Then instruct your dragon to light a fire of hope and optimism, and burn the things you can't use until everything is ash.

Now sprinkle this rich ash across the garden. Before you open your eyes, imagine how this rich mulch has helped your Field of Dreams grow with purpose and beauty.

Choose one object from the remaining pile. Then open your eyes.

Begin part two of the exercise: Using your drawing, painting, or sculpting supplies, draw a picture of what that one remaining object represents, or create a sculpture about it. If you prefer, you can write a poem or song about it, dance a dance that expresses it, or just say a few words about who you have become as a result of it.

Be creative and allow inspiration to move you to create the symbol of your experience or to create a work of art from it. What you create will represent your wisdom crystalized into a sacred talisman, an object of symbolism to show how you've been shaped by your past and empowered to move forward into the uncharted places of the Map waiting to be discovered.

I said earlier that the Realm of Light is the realm where you transform the old, but it's also where you create something new, informed by what you learned and the wisdom you acquired when doing the work in the Realm of Mind. In the Realm of Light, you start to conceive of how you can work differently with the energies here, the memories and emotions and information. The sadness and the story can turn into a country song! The memory of suffering can become the memory of survival and triumph that you share with others to help them heal. The memory can simply become something that you hold on to but rarely think about, and when you do, it has no power over you.

We all signed up for spiritual narcolepsy, so we must journey to rediscover the light—to write a new story and evolve so that we can co-create what we desire. We all are here to experience life on life's terms, and that means accepting the sadness, the pain, the disappointment, and the frustration. What we don't have to do is suffer over our suffering, exacerbating it. Doing that puts us back into the Ghostlands of the past where nothing new can be created. It's better to repurpose the treasure, finding new ways to work with it—and play with it! We do that when we let ourselves feel childlike wonder as we open up to all the many ways to interpret and work with what we find in the shadow. Blow off the dust and cobwebs that lie atop the treasure and discover it anew. Release any fear, shame, or sorrow that obscures the view of that magical treasure. As the light comes in, you'll see that the treasure glitters, sending out rainbow colors that dance all around you.

INTEGRATION OF WHAT YOU RECLAIMED

What energy, quality, or aspect of yourself did you reclaim during the exercise earlier? Was it a wild and free rebel, a dancer, or a teacher? It may have been your gentle, feminine self, your brave warrior, your unapologetic outsider, or your playful child. What form did it take? It's good to journal about your impressions after an exercise like this one and to be on the lookout for messages from Spirit that will give you even more insights about that aspect of who you are and how to integrate it into your life.

It's also good to act as if that self were already fully integrated, like a child playing "let's pretend." Acting as if you already are that new, integrated self may feel uncomfortable or awkward at first—you may fall on your face like I did the first time I drove a motorcycle. But you have to let yourself tolerate the strange feeling that this isn't really you. Use your imagination and pretend, as you did when you were a child playing with your friends and your toys.

There are many ways to act "as if" you have fully integrated a part of yourself that you're reclaiming. My editor, Nancy, bought herself roses and a heart-shaped box of chocolates one Valentine's Day as a way of rehearsing the woman who received these sorts of gifts from her lover and felt entitled to enjoy them. She did find the man of her dreams, and yes, that scene she imagined plays out every Valentine's Day. I'm not saying that the Law of Attraction always operates like this; as you'll learn in Chapter 10, the romantic energy you create within can be reflected in form in different ways, not necessarily in the way you expect.

In the Realm of Light, as I said, you might find parts of yourself that aren't serving you anymore: the beliefs, memories, and emotions that you placed in deep storage. Looking at them anew with the light of insight, you can see that they may have helped you in the past. Be grateful for that. But if you don't need them anymore, let go of them. They're clutter.

The light allows us to fully accept the small self with all its warts, and to acknowledge Spirit as being all, and to say, "Let me love that part of me instead of hating it or shaming or denying it." Then opportunities appear because you've turned the light on. That's what the Total Mindshift Process is all about—turning on the light so you can look within and work differently with the treasures in your shadow.

I am using metaphors here, but the energies I'm talking about are powerful and *real.* Once on New Year's Eve, I was with friends, and we passed around a talking stick. I could see the diaphanous light surrounding the stick, swirling around my friends, and igniting a comet of electric sparks that arced across the space between them and dissipated into the roiling energy that enveloped us all. Never forget that you, like everyone, are a being of light, spirit, and mind, integrated into the energetic matrix of creation. The energies that are a part of your energy field are integrated into your body, into your very cells, as well as your consciousness. You may not see them or feel them easily, but they are there, and you can learn the skill of sensing them along with the skill of working with them. In the next chapter, you'll find practical ways to do this and learn how to work with the energy you have discovered within.

Traveler's Notes

- The Realm of Light is where you connect with the light energy of Spirit, who knows and sees all, even what is in the dark corners of your awareness—and loves every part of you.
- In the Realm of Light you do a fearless inventory and consciously choose what to reclaim and what to discard as well as what to repurpose.
- Also in the Realm of Light, you begin to reprogram the subconscious so that it stores memories differently and attaches new emotional energy to them.
- Your task in the Realm of Light is to practice radical acceptance and forgiveness of yourself and others. This is the place of freedom and creativity.
- Because light shining upon an object always casts a shadow, in the Realm of Light you have to face some darkness. You illumine parts of yourself you see as ugly and shameful, but you observe that these qualities can also be positive.
- In the Realm of Light, you start to conceive of how you can work differently with the memories and emotions and information in your subconscious.
- If you do not enter the Realm of Light, but instead try to skip ahead to co-create something new, you may find yourself stuck in Ghostlands, where you fall back into the old patterns and nothing new can come to be.

9

THE REALM OF ENERGY

Now you have illuminated the dark corners of your awareness and reclaimed the forgotten parts of yourself. Now the multi-dimensional Map of your soul has been revealed and your eyes have opened to the glow of silvery pathways that lead you to new opportunities and yet-to-be-discovered potential. Now the past makes so much more sense. Your soul, which thinks in terms of experiences, themes, and collaboration, at last understands you have been on the journey of co-creative evolution to find your purpose and authentic self all along. If you stick with it, using the process of co-creative evolution, you will end up where you most want to be, having the experiences you yearn to have and some you had no idea you would love so much.

Spirit has blessed you with the power to co-write your story rather than be tossed about by the winds of fate. Carl Jung, when he said, "Whatever is not brought from the unconscious into conscious awareness seemingly comes to us as fate," understood that unless we get beyond the limitations of the small mind, we are going to have limited power over our lives.

To experience the uncharted places as magical rather than threatening, you have to work with the longings of your soul and stop ignoring its messages to your small mind. Life doesn't work out so well when you stifle that authentic inner voice. At this moment, you might not be sure what story you want to write, and you might have doubts about whether it can come to life. But believe me, here in the Realm of Energy, the magic of the uncharted starts to make itself felt in a big way.

The work you did in the Realm of Light leads you naturally to the Realm of Energy. Here is where ideas, epiphanies, inspired thought forms, the light of understanding, and your intention to co-create something new commingle and become infused with life-force energy before coalescing into form. The task now is to learn to steward and direct the energies mindfully instead of feeling powerless to do anything but surrender to their currents—although there are times when trusting the currents is exactly what you must do, especially when you've entered choppier waters.

ENERGY 101: WHAT YOU HAVE TO KNOW

The true nature of the universe is energetic. Science tells us that at the subatomic level, even matter is energy if you expect it to be: Due to the observer effect, if you expect to see a wave of light, you will, but if you expect the microscope to show you a particle, that's what you will see. Perception is what solidifies light into matter.

Before there is form, there is consciousness, light, and energy. Working with all those before working with form is important. You wouldn't just get into your car, start the engine, put it into drive, and hit the gas—you'd move forward, yes, but you'd probably drive right into the wall of the garage! You need an intention, a plan, and some preparatory work before taking a trip. The same is true when you've stepped into uncharted territory. The preparation is faith; the plan is invoking Spirit, holding your intention loosely, remaining curious, and allowing the soul's Map to be revealed as you find your true steps. Learning to maintain a stable energy regardless of temporary outer conditions that were set in motion by your past self is key to this co-creative evolutionary process. The work of the interconnected realms is not yet complete, so don't rush to the Realm of Form to try to manifest and attract all that your small mind thinks you want for yourself.

KNOWING HOW ENERGY WORKS HELPS YOU WORK WITH IT

The nature of the universe is energy, and the form the energy takes is constantly evolving. Energy can't be created or destroyed, as Einstein explained. It can only change form. When it does, you have to accept the loss, which can be very hard to do. Loss generates grief, anger, resentment, jealousy, fear—ouch! Ah, but on the other side, you signed up for this. It was spiritual amnesia that made you forget how very real suffering feels when you're human. The comfort is in knowing that using the co-creative process of evolution with the Map of your soul as your guide reduces *unnecessary* suffering and softens its intensity.

That doesn't mean you will not suffer ever—just that you won't suffer over your suffering. When you are aware and conscious of your energy, you can recognize the beauty within some forms of suffering when it happens and see how it can make meaningful and profound shifts in your life. When you experience grief when a beloved pet dies, you can recognize how the pain you're feeling is not just loss but the breaking open and expanding of your heart, as you have more love as a result of the relationship. Anger can be initiated in victimization but then transmuted and used to galvanize others to make changes in a situation of inequity. Jealousy can remind you that your thoughts have moved away from abundance. Being aware of energy and how it works allows you to create something new—something that may even be better than what you had before.

To do this last step in the preparation for working in the Realm of Form, stay connected to the Realm of Spirit, which connects the other four co-creative realms from above. Spirit's help in directing energy is invaluable—and Spirit will comfort you and bolster your courage and confidence as you continue working with this process of co-creative evolution. Think of Spirit as that service where you can just push a button and say, "Where am I?" and hear a comforting disembodied voice that can tell you your exact location and what to do next.

One of Spirit's great gifts to all is omnipresence: Spirit is always there to help you steward energy with your intention and through actions that match your intentions rather than your will (more on intention versus will a little later). It's the small self that steers you in the wrong direction, down the path of least resistance and conformity or holding an identity as a victim; it's the small self that holds tight in rebellious resistance to change.

One of my biggest joys in doing readings is that in connecting to the other side, I can see potential in people that they've shut down in themselves. I'll tell the person I'm reading for, "I see and sense that what you really want to do is [work with animals, become a photographer, go back to school and study to become a psychologist or social worker, or whatever it is]," and watch the person's face light up—because that deepest desire has been brought to the surface. People have so many passions buried in the shadows that need to come into the light. Jesus said we should not hide our light under a bushel—that's exactly what people do because of fear and shame. And that's why if you were too scared to actually do the work in the Realm of Light illuminating those dark corners, you're cheating yourself.

If you have taken the time to explore the qualities found within you—however ugly or embarrassing or intimidating they might seem—and brought them into the light, you have reclaimed lost parts of yourself. Acknowledging their influence is the first step in freeing yourself from the fear and shame and anger that constricted you. Now you have to release those emotional energies, along with the inspiration, creativity, and passion that got stuck within your energy field and your body, so it can express itself in the world. All that energy you expended squashing your desire to move, paint, speak your truth, sing, write, or express who you really are, will be freed up too.

Your energy is shifting as you step into the Realm of Energy, and your small mind is being flooded with the realization that it really is okay to let go of the old story and what once served you but no longer does. You might need to give up a relationship with someone you love deeply, or release your image of yourself as this and not that, but you can tolerate the emotional turmoil and the losses. There are many different "deaths" you have to experience in this life, and let's face it, all of them hurt. But while we're here in human form, we have to accept that death and endings are a part of life. Nothing is ever wasted. Everything is recycled and repurposed, and after death there is a rebirth and a renewal. It helps to know that every moment offers an opportunity for returning to the Realm of Spirit and becoming renewed. Again and again, you can return to the process of co-creation and to the magical, uncharted places on your soul's Map. This is the Map that will help you to rise above the pain and dull its sting. Remember that in the uncharted, the treasure of your greatest potential is waiting to be discovered.

ENERGY, EMOTION, AND ENERGY IN MOTION

Participate with Spirit in co-creating something new and you will be healing old wounds and freeing up your personal power at the same time. Yes, that dragon is being let out of the dungeon to take a spin around the kingdom with you at the reins!

The old anger or shame you've been carrying far too long can dissipate as you release old emotional energies and say good-bye to the stories of failure or inadequacy. However, I know that finding a new perspective on what happened can be much easier than letting go of your feelings. Emotions have energy and even a physical reality in your body as you generate and experience them and as they move through you. An emotion instantly sparks biochemical reactions that set off physical symptoms you can notice if you tune in to how you feel in your body when you're upset. That's been shown by science. In fact, scientific researcher Candace Pert revolutionized her field by discovering that emotions create biochemical compounds called peptides that serve as messengers in the brain; her team's work won the prestigious Albert Lasker Award, which is often a precursor to the Nobel Prize.

You're supposed to feel emotions temporarily and then let them flow through you and out of you so they don't become stuck in your cells and tissues. Memories are emotions intertwined with thoughts, and those can become lodged not just in your brain but in your body too. There are different hypotheses about how exactly this works, but Candace Pert explains that memories can be found stored biochemically in the synapses where neurons (brain cells) connect to each other: "The sensitivity of the receptors are part of memory and pattern storage," she said in a 1995 interview with Lynn Grodzki, LCSW, that appeared in *Pathways* magazine. But, she added, "the peptide network extends beyond the hippocampus, to organs, tissue, skin, muscle and endocrine glands. They all have peptides receptors on them and can access and store emotional information. This means the emotional memory is stored in many places in the body, not just the brain. The autonomic nervous system is pivotal to this entire understanding." The autonomic nervous system is where you experience the cascade of physical reactions to your emotions—it's the system that switches hormones on and off, changes your breathing and heart-rate patterns, and more in response to fear and stress.

Even if you haven't studied the science of how energy affects and forms patterns in the physical world, you have experienced it, as I have. Once, I ran into an old friend with whom I had severed ties years before. My relationship with this person had been constantly in chaos, unhealthy, and not serving either of us, so we had grown apart. I had tremendous anxiety whenever I was around this friend, triggered by the friend's history of anger and my history around abuse. Over and over, I found myself back experiencing the energy of my 19-year-old self and the rape, when I couldn't defend myself and capitulated out of fear. After the friendship ended, I rarely thought about this person, and I assumed I had simply moved on, but when I saw this person approaching on the sidewalk, I felt a sense of panic and quickly crossed the street. I asked myself, "When am I?" (not where but *when*) and realized I wasn't present in the now; I was experiencing the energy of the past. Deep breathing and tuning in to the Observer reconnected me to my soul and small self. I imagined myself in the hand of God, surrounded by love and light, and I sent my former friend the intention of compassion. The nightmare ended as the energy in my body shifted. I was no longer disempowered by the stored energy that had infused the memory.

When our dog Beanie died, Marc and I grieved deeply. At the same time, I completely lost my hearing in my left ear. I went to three specialists who put me through all kinds of tests, and no one could tell me why I lost my hearing. Energy healer and chiropractic doctor Dr. Darren Weissman had helped me before with his miraculous LifeLine Technique, so I called him and he was able to take me through a process over the phone to release the grief from my body that also released a stored memory of something that had happened to me when I was four years old. It was extraordinary how the energy swept through my body as he helped me release it through infinite love and gratitude. My entire body tingled and vibrated as we went through the process. I woke up the next day with my hearing intact after 31 days of being completely deaf in that ear. This is just one example of the intersection of the Realms of Mind and Energy. Subconscious automatic programs are actually stored in the body and activated when events line up to trigger a past memory you might not even know you have.

So while you may still be eager to get into the Realm of Form and fix what's "wrong" with your life, I think you now have an even better grasp of why you're going through this process of co-creative evolution, step to step, realm to realm. When you enter the Realm of Energy, Spirit helps you loosen your restrictions and release all those stuck energies. That opens up space for new energies to rush into your personal energy field. What might rush in? Courage, radical creativity and inspiration, assertiveness, gentleness and compassion, and yes, love.

Energies such as confidence, joy, and nurturance that exist as archetypes in the matrix come into you through the membrane that is your soul. They affect your body and your cells, moving them like the wind moves the surface of the ocean, forming waves, or like the underground currents move the water and the particles within it. You also can think of the Realm of Energy as the realm of motion, where the soul's intention that has been forming becomes unleashed and begins to affect form. In the Realm of Mind, you learned about acting "as if" so you could begin to train your subconscious mind to be in sync with your conscious desires. In the

Realm of Light, you took the bold step of shedding light on your story and the dark places of your awareness where you had hidden what made you uncomfortable. Now it will be easier to take actions in sync with your intention without being tripped up by energies in your subconscious because you are working with archetypal forces consciously. You'll be mindfully stewarding the energy available to you, using your intuition to dialogue with Spirit for guidance, and readying yourself to experience the manifestation of your intention in the Realm of Form.

INTENTION IS WISER THAN WILL

Positive, creative intention is desire generated by the soul. It doesn't automatically ignore the desires of the small self; it listens, and it will incorporate them to some degree. The soul isn't attached to form, so the desire for abundance that your small mind has conceptualized as a desire to have money flow into your bank account right now may end up as the intention to simply open to and attract more abundance in all its many forms.

Your intuition can guide you well when you're setting an intention. You might say, "That's what I want," but feel, *No, that's not good for me.* I did a lot of manifesting of opportunities and financial abundance when I was working as an intuitive strategist and business coach, but my intuition was telling me I was supposed to experience abundance differently—in a way that didn't sacrifice my soul's calling to use my gift of communicating with spirits who have passed. The energy wasn't flowing, and I sensed it.

Surrendering to the authentic truth about who I am and being transparent to myself about it was hugely impactful. I still do intuitive business coaching and strategic planning for a few ongoing, select clients, but I'm no longer trying to fit into a box, nor trying to suppress any other part of my abilities anymore. Those clients know about everything I do and they love it. I am not for everyone, but that's a good thing now. I hide nothing, and that is a powerful freedom and not one I take for granted.

Your soul forms intention with the influence of Spirit. When the small self remembers your true nature as a spiritual being, the subconscious, which operates from memory, opens up to the unconscious, which communicates easily with Spirit via the soul. Then your soul's wisdom is fully accessible and you're open to even greater wisdom than your own. If the small self is smart, it will choose to surrender to the greater wisdom of Spirit and pray, "Thy will be done." Intention is properly made up of individual will, soul intention, and the intention of Spirit in alignment.

Earlier, I explained that the soul is an energy body encasing your own body and brain and woven into the consciousness of your cells, including your brain cells and neural networks, while at the same time being woven into the matrix. Your soul is the membrane, the container for your individual awareness, and the conduit to Spirit and all of Spirit's wisdom. The small mind, in contrast, draws its knowledge from its experiences in this lifetime—from the familiar. It has a lot of knowledge and even some wisdom, as it's learned and evolved along the way, and can access this when it's in a state of integration. However, on its own, it's very limited in what it can understand, and in the uncharted places, it feels lost. The small self's thoughts, plans, and choices—its will—can lead you to some very uncomfortable places on the Map. When energy is moving rapidly, the small self may want to resist that with great fervor—much as some fundamentalists would rather see us all back in the Dark Ages. The small self's will is powerful in terms of its ability to decide and choose, and perseverance toward a goal is good, but will in excess is much overrated.

The Lord's Prayer says, "Thy will be done." One of my favorite affirmations is "Thy will be done through me." Your soul, which is able to receive Spirit's guidance and wisdom, is much smarter than your small mind, which is the source of your personal will. Think of an inspired intention as your soul's will combined with the plans, ambitions, and desires of your small self. It's not that your small self doesn't have some good ideas. It is an expression of Divine Love, a detail in the great work of art created by the Creator. You, me, and all of us are the painter and the painted, the dancer and the danced, the writer and the character in the story we co-write with Spirit. "Thy will" is not out of sync with the longings of each individual soul. On the contrary, "Thy will" is filled with joy when we stop resisting those longings and sync up with Spirit and all who participate in our sparkling dance of creation.

CO-CREATING THROUGH THE LAW OF ATTRACTION

As a being of light and energy, you are constantly sending out messages to the universe. The HeartMath Institute has conducted and collected research demonstrating that even though our brains use most of our body's fuel, it's our hearts that send out the greatest amount of energy. According to research, the energy field of your heart extends several feet outward from your chest. That is one powerful energetic release that you want to be able to direct through your intention, because in response to this energy message you release, the universe responds with situations and people whose energy is a match for you. That, in short, is the Law of Attraction.

The challenge is to make sure the energy you are drawing in and the energy you are sending outward (without trying) is what you want it to be. Can you tell what its qualities are? To send out the energetic message of joy, abundance, and kindness is far better than sending out an energetic message of panic or scarcity. Use your intention instead of your will, and the energetic messages will be less likely to have the qualities you don't want. Intention can only be created when you wake up out of spiritual narcolepsy and let your soul and not your small self lead you.

Do you remember that sequence in Walt Disney's *Fantasia* called "The Sorcerer's Apprentice"? The great sorcerer in his blue robe and starry pointed cap manipulates the forces of magic easily and powerfully. When he settles in for a nap, Mickey Mouse, his apprentice, tripping over his own robe and trying to keep the pointed cap from slipping and covering his eyes, is convinced he's able to handle the same work his mentor can. But the power turns out to be too much for him to control. That's what happens when the small self fools itself into thinking it's got things handled—it's really the subconscious and its irrational impulses and memory-based emotions that have been in charge. It's humbling, frightening, and overwhelming to realize just how much you have *not* been handling a challenging situation.

In *Fantasia*, the sorcerer wakes up in time to take charge and clean up the disaster Mickey Mouse has set into motion. Phew! Your own soul can wake up and clean up the disasters your small self creates. But if you make a habit of orienting yourself in the Realm of Spirit instead of rushing forward to fix your life and make everything happen your way or the highway in the Realm of Form, using your will, the magic of the uncharted places will delight you instead of scare you—and you won't have to do so much cleanup.

As for that bit about "Man plans, God laughs," remember, you're always on your soul's path even if you can't see where you're going or recall why you traveled on such a winding road. Energy always moves forward and will carry you where you want to go. That's true of your soul's path too—but the road is spiraling, just like the path of the Milky Way galaxy through our universe. Patterns repeat themselves, but the ideal is for them to be patterns of opportunity for change, not patterns of repetitive suffering. The difference between the two is your perception.

So how do you move with this energy, guiding it as you immerse yourself in it? You do it by setting your intention and visualizing something different. At first, you act as if it were true, as I said earlier. Then, and only then, do you take action, because your small self has stepped back and let your soul speak to you through your first sense—intuition. Now the actions you take will be right for you. Your messages to the universe will be in sync with your soul's longings and any interference from your subconscious will be minimized because your soul, guided by Spirit, is steering. The right use of will is in alignment with Spirit and in service to the highest good. The right use of will is stewardship, guiding but not forcing and certainly not dominating. Rarely does force produce the results you truly desire. And those results have a tendency to quickly disintegrate when you remove the force. Your soul will always steer you into a new experience, and your intuition will be a useful navigational tool.

THE FIRST SENSE: INTUITION

As I mentioned earlier in the book, intuition gets called the sixth sense—as if it's not as trustworthy as the five senses of sight, hearing, taste, smell, and touch—but intuition is really your first sense. And intuition is your guide in working with energy, so you have to learn to tune in to it. That requires letting go of your skepticism and simply accepting that there are ways of knowing things without having evidence right in front of you. When you find you know something—in fact, you're certain of it—but can't explain why, don't dismiss the feeling as irrational and irrelevant. Become quiet and don't pay any attention to the words that form in your mind and start turning into a wave of thoughts that will carry you away. The chatterbox inside you can yammer away all it likes—don't give it weight or importance. Just be quietly present with it, and observe what images or sensations come to you. If you sense a message has come from Spirit, *listen.*

Intuition gets honed by spiritual practice, a regular pattern of actions that work to put you in touch with your intuition and messages from your soul and from Spirit. Thinking about how you ought to meditate or journal won't cut it. Your gas tank doesn't get filled just because you know where the gas station is! Spiritual practice is the same. To keep the lines of communication with Spirit open, slow down and open up to feeling and sensing your connection. You can meditate, which I mentioned earlier, or do tapping, or walk on the beach and listen to the waves, or do yoga or Reiki—whatever helps you to feel and experience Spirit and your intuition.

Oracles, whether they are cards you use or symbols you work with (like my dragonfly), are tools for developing and dialoguing with Spirit by honing your intuition. There are many different ideas about how they work, but the simplest explanation is that you open to Spirit, ask a question, and then let Spirit guide you to choose a card—or let Spirit send you a sign. Interpretations of signs and cards are very personal, even though there are some universal understandings about what they symbolize. A red-winged blackbird suddenly swooping in front of you can mean you are on the right track and should move forward, but to someone else, it can simply mean it's that time of the year when the red-winged blackbirds are in the area to nest. The universe has consciousness within it, but there is randomness as well. So is it a sign, or just a bird flying past? Listen to your intuition to find out!

And if it *is* a sign, an oracle, what is its message? We are the ones who bring the meaning to symbols. Yes, we project our own understanding onto them—that's the point. As long as your understanding isn't forced (like when I was trying to convince myself that a housefly counted as a dragonfly) and is coming from your intuition, you can trust it. You might not understand the message at first, but sit with it.

When you use oracle cards for predictions, you open up to the possible meanings of the signs and allow the energy to coalesce into form. Be mindful of warnings and act accordingly. There's no need to fear a reversed card as a "bad" card that's usually thought to indicate a challenge. I refer to them in my decks as protection cards, and I even began creating them with clear directives about how to avoid trouble! In fact, you're just getting a message that the energy is not moving in the direction you would like it to, so you should be cautious and try to consciously connect to other energies you can steward and direct like the current of a stream.

Omens are not fixed. They portend a possibility or probability of a synchronicity that will come together to form an event or series of events that you might prefer to change. They're always offering you information that, when acted upon accordingly, can lead to a situation that may be better. All oracles speak to the energies that are flowing through your story and the stories that influence and intersect with yours at any given time. Energy is always fluid, and it serves as a moving mirror on the journey.

EFFECTIVE STEWARDING OF ENERGY

In the Realm of Light, you need to be mindful of the energy that is affecting you and work with it consciously. If you are often distracted and allowing energy to dissipate, you're not being a very effective steward. Where is your energy going? What is your internal dialogue like: Does it support your intention to have healthy beliefs and cause you to feel optimistic or happy, or does it make you feel tired or anxious? Track the activities and relationships you are spending your time and energy on and observe whether that's in sync with what you want for yourself. Meditation on the body is a way to get grounded and build greater control over "energy leakage" and your internal dialogue.

Taking your awareness off your thoughts and directing it toward your body and your first sense, intuition, helps you to become conscious of your energy, which is an important step in learning to manage it. The following exercise can help too.

Exercise: Body Scan

Scanning your body to see where energy may be stuck and needs to be released is a simple technique you can use to steward energy effectively.

First, sit comfortably, relax, and breathe deeply and slowly. Tune in to the Observer within you and imagine that this Observer hovers a foot outside of what you perceive to be the boundary of your physical form. Ask yourself these three questions:

Where in my body am I contracted?
Where in my body am I neutral?
Where in my body am I expansive?

Now draw your attention to the soles of your feet. You will feel it right away as your awareness scans your energy. You might begin by sensing whether your feet are neutral or have a tense area, such as a tight spot in your arch. When you discover an area of your body is neutral, bless this area with gratitude and respect. Then, when you come to a place that feels expansive, allow that energy to move to areas you've just brought gratitude and respect to. And when you come to a place of contraction, imagine you are flooding that area with light and life-force energy, breathing deeply until you reach a neutral zone. Why you're contracted in that area isn't important. Stay out of the story of what happened when and why, or you'll actually anchor the energy there so it can't move freely. Just observe the constricted spot and fill it with an expansive, loving energy. Now you can observe your situation with detachment and let it go.

Continue the body scan, working your way up your body, observing the spots that are neutral, constricted, or expansive, and switching the energies as instructed. When you've finished scanning the area at the top of your head, you're finished and can open your eyes.

After a forgotten part of you that needed reclaiming has been brought to light and you have become aware of it once again, you can reintegrate its energy into your life. You can acknowledge the part of you that was vocal and insisted that you deserved to have what you wanted, and you can let it speak without being afraid that someone might get offended or think you are too bossy or self-centered. That dragon of your personal power has been reclaimed and tamed!

What's the energy in your surroundings? You want the space you live or work in to have spots that are calming and spots that are energizing. Feeling that you don't belong there or that the energy is disturbed can drain you. Keep the space clear of clutter as well, as each piece of clutter chatters away with a story. Can you imagine the cacophony of influences that arise out of a room full of clutter?

Once, someone gave me a vase I felt obliged to keep, but every time I looked at it, I felt her controlling, edgy, critical energy. The vase triggered the energy of those qualities in me. Why would I want to do that to myself on a daily basis? I gave the vase to someone who loved it and who now connects it to a story of my generosity instead. In the same way, clothes that tell you how fat you are or how ridiculous you are for spending so much money on them need to go. It doesn't help the flow of energy in your life one bit when you have something that will work for you "maybe one day." If it doesn't make you feel great when you look at it, get rid of it. The energy changes when you replace the item with something else or leave the space empty to be filled with something better. Sometimes empty is better.

You can alter the energy of space by how you arrange and decorate it. Classical feng shui expert Angel de Para, whom I introduced you to earlier, works with me to change the energy in my home on every new moon cycle. We feel the energy shift immediately when we do this. The ancient art of feng shui is all about working with objects in physical space to better steward the energy that is always flowing through your home, your yard, and your office. Even if you don't use classical feng shui, at the very least tune in to how you feel in the spaces where you spend large amounts of time and try to make them in sync with energies you want in your life: freedom, creativity, abundance, happiness, humor, whatever it is you would like to influence and surround you. That's a good way to start working with energy: by inviting it in.

Stewarding energy involves bringing in the forces that can serve you and sweep away the old stuff you don't want anymore, like resentment or beliefs about not being worthy of what you want for yourself. It also involves conscious direction of energy and releasing energy that doesn't serve you or that has gotten stuck in your energy field, slowing you down and creating an obstacle.

You bring in energies when you reclaim aspects of yourself, but the idea is to work with those energies differently. You don't have to be innocent and trusting in a way that attracts people who hurt you and sends you retreating into familiar places. You can be strong as well as open—alert to who is worthy of your trust and who has energy that is not in sync with your soul's longing. If you want to experience your childlike innocence again without the hurt and betrayal, you can bring in the energy of love and compassion.

You also want to draw in replenishing energy overall. Restorative sleep, good healthy food, time with those you love, basking in sunlight, enjoying the outdoors, being around positive people, moving your body—all are ways to bring in new energy. You can't live on positive thoughts. You have a body, and it needs care!

And your energy field needs to be replenished with energy that is of a high frequency, that is, energy with a high vibratory rate. If you and I as energy beings have a similar vibrational frequency, we resonate with each other and are attracted to each other. Change your vibrational frequency and you're not going to be attracted to the same people and situations anymore except out of habit. The emotional "charge" will no longer be there when you find yourself in a familiar place. You see the exit ramp marked "destructive relationship" and feel no compulsion to put on your turn signal.

RELEASING OR DISCHARGING ENERGY

When it comes to stewarding energy, releasing energy is just as important as drawing it in. You don't want to become overstimulated by all the energy in you—you have to be able to rest. And if you have too much of a particular energy, let go of some of it. Being loving and nurturing is wonderful, but caretaking for everyone all the time will exhaust you and overwhelm others. Let energy flow through you, or that excess energy can keep you up at night or get stuck in your body and cause problems. Having porous boundaries and taking in too much energy, even positive energy, can disorient you. When I do a lot of readings in a row, I can become so overwhelmed I can hardly think, and I have to take a nap—or I start to reach for sugary, fattening foods like cookies in an attempt to ground myself in my body and remember where I end and other people begin. We may be energy beings, but we're not master stewards of energy, and it's easy to take in far more than you can handle emotionally and mentally.

Releasing or discharging energy puts you into a state of balance, which is something we naturally seek on our co-evolutionary journey: a balance between action and rest, between stimulation and quiet, hustle and flow, between our needs and others' needs. In the story of the Three Bears, Goldilocks wanted the chair, the bed, and the porridge to be "just right." In mythology, Daedalus, father of Icarus, made wax-and-feather wings for himself and his son to fly to their freedom: he warned Icarus not to fly too high, where the sun would melt his wings, or too low, where the ocean's dampness might make the wings too heavy, causing him to fall into the sea and drown. Instinctively, we know that we are meant to find a "just right" balance between extremes.

When you honor your need for rest, you maintain the energy to continue working toward the manifestation of your intention. When you balance your time for reflecting and connecting in love to Spirit, you gain mental clarity and clear out the emotional debris that gets in your way. But if you don't create balance, you end up in familiar places where you experience the pain of your old wounds. You think you're going forward and whoops, your winding path turns out to be circular, taking you right back to where you were before.

To manifest what you desire, you have to balance giving and receiving, or being in a state of motion and being in a state of reception. And balance is always in flux, never static, so when I say *balance*, I'm talking about bringing the wild swings of thought, energy, and motion into a semblance of calm, avoiding excess in all areas of life. Say no to drama. Make your life a no-drama zone and you'll be so happy you did. Self-care is critical in these changing times. If your own well is dry, how can you be generous with others? You'll have nothing to give!

"Just right" action—or as Buddhists call it, Right Action—is action that is only undertaken mindfully. You remain mindful of Spirit, of your spiritual nature, and of the balance between action and flow. And you avoid distractions—the thoughts, situations, and relationships that keep you running and juggling and constantly in motion. When your intuition calls to you and your small self is tempted to shut down its inconvenient messages, slow down and listen. After that, the action you take will turn out to be the right one.

Track your energy. We live surrounded by the temptation to distract ourselves and have the habit of multitasking, giving partial energy to everything. Draw it in, direct it intentionally, and release energy out in the world to discharge it or set in motion the waves of change in the Realm of Form—which is where we're going next.

Ram Dass said, "You and I are the force for transformation in the world. We are the consciousness that will define the nature of the reality we are moving into." It is when we engage with the interconnected Realms of Spirit, Mind, Light, Energy, and Form that the transformation essential to our survival and our joy in being here becomes possible. What reality are you creating? What can we co-create together?

Traveler's Notes

- In the Realm of Energy, ideas and intention become infused with energy that you direct consciously so it can coalesce into form.
- Stewarding energy involves releasing it as well as drawing it in.
- You don't want to become overstimulated by all the energy in you—you have to be able to rest.
- Remember that you are co-creating, living between the pillars of what you can change and what you can't, but using the Map of your soul as your guide reduces *unnecessary* suffering and softens its intensity.
- In the Realm of Energy it is important to release emotional energies, letting go of what you don't need, bringing in the inspiration, creativity, and passion that have been stuck and unable to flow through you.
- You must release the energy of your emotions, which can be more difficult than simply finding a new perspective on what happened, because emotions have energy and even a physical reality in your body.
- Intention is, properly, made up of individual will, soul intention, and the intention of Spirit, all in alignment with one another.

- In the Realm of Energy, you sync up with Spirit and all who participate in our sparkling dance of creation.
- Do not force matters—this rarely produces desirable results.
- Avoid excess in all areas of life. Say no to drama.
- Thinking about how you ought to meditate or journal to get in touch with Spirit won't cut it. Your gas tank doesn't get filled just because you know where the gas station is!

10

THE REALM OF FORM

In the Realm of Form, co-creation happens tangibly. You have transformed internally as a result of taking the journey of self-discovery, and you have become the change you want to see in your world. You have become the person you need to be to have the experiences you want to have. Can you hold on to that self, or will you flee to the comfort of familiarity? There's always a temptation to return to the old habits, but it's so much easier to resist now that you have done the work of the previous realms.

So now you are entering the last stretch of the spiraling inward journey across the uncharted waters of new opportunities and infinite potential. You are about to land on the shore of a new frontier. But then you recognize that you have always been here, at all times—on the soft, sparkling sands of greatness and creativity and wondrous possibilities for your existence here on earth. You've never *not* been here! And as you stay tuned to Spirit and see through the perfectly calibrated lens of integrated soul and small self, you know you've been invited into this sacred, excruciating, miraculous unfolding by a Love that knows no bounds. This Love loves you so much it forces you to keep moving, to let what is no longer needed go, no matter how painful it is to feel the energy again as it loosens up and flows out of you like cathartic tears. All of it—the fear, uncertainty, courage, and elation—were part of the journey inward you had to take to get to the core of who you're really meant to be. Now you can add your Light to the sum of all Light to help us all find home.

When you move your attention to the Realm of Form after working your way through the others (instead of plopping yourself there first, as you used to), you'll see how everything has come together in a perfect dance. Ideas that existed as potentialities in the Realm of Mind have already met up with the insights you discovered in the Realm of Light. Courageously exploring the landscape of that realm, you shined the light on parts of yourself and your story that needed to be recovered, repurposed, and healed. That was necessary for personal transformation. All those insights and concepts moved forward like a ball of light into the Realm of Energy, where you stewarded the energy to write a new story of personal evolution that could coalesce in the Realm of Form. Intention and motivation have been like a gentle, warm wind that's deposited you softly on the ground here in the Realm of Form—and it feels good.

Acquiring deep insights into yourself and taming the dragons that triggered your inner fears has brought you power and wisdom. You now know that magic is not an abstract notion made of airy-fairy dust but as real as can be. A wish that carried upward into the sky on the feathery wings of a dandelion seed has landed on the earth, and it's *you*, ready to take root in the Realm of Form, stretch to the sky, and blossom.

The work takes far less effort now than it did when you were in this realm before, thinking that the way to change your life was to be relentlessly ambitious and plan harder, work harder, overanalyze, restrict and control, and cross your fingers that the fates would smile kindly on you. Where once you had to force things to happen, now you are in the flow of the Divine—yet your feet are firmly planted on the ground. There is no longer a separation between the spiritual and the physical realm. You see how they are interwoven on the Map of the soul. Spirituality isn't only experienced when you're alone meditating or praying. It's a part of your everyday life, influencing your perceptions and choices—and how you store memories.

And at last your will, your soul's intent, and Divine Will are in alignment, working together, and you see the results of that alignment in your life. The Law of Attraction is in operation, and the universe is starting to reflect your new story and your higher vibration. It is catching up to where you are inside, rearranging itself to reflect the new you and what you've co-created within. There's still work to be done, but now you're cruising almost effortlessly.

And what you wish to create for yourself may have changed dramatically. You've come to see the pros and cons of any situation or relationship, and with that clarity, you can make much better decisions about what to keep and what to discard. The emotional drama and mental confusion has lifted, and you feel lighter—even effervescent.

What surrounds you will look familiar in many ways, but you'll see it with new eyes because *you* have changed. Your understanding is deeper because Spirit has infused all with meaning and now you get it. You can finally see why you went from here to there, why you suffered that terrible loss and those turbulent waters of uncertainty. If all that hadn't transpired, you wouldn't be here with a new sense of who you are and who you can be. Nothing you experienced was wasted. You now know that what you've been through will help you be a more loving and compassionate person, a wiser teacher, or a more intuitive and skilled healer. You have mastered the art of co-creative evolution, and you no longer have to fear the process of transformation or the changes that are thrust on you. When the spiritual narcolepsy kicks in, you will be asleep to your spiritual nature for much shorter periods, and you'll easily return to an integrated state with soul and small self in partnership collaborating on behalf of Spirit.

Because you will have done the work of self-evolution, you will feel comfortable in your own skin and in the life you have chosen for yourself. Remember that the essence of your intention and desire is more important than the form. The form it takes will be up to Spirit, and it likely will manifest in unexpected and surprising ways. When you experience the manifestation and see how it all works, your multidimensional Map of the soul will shift yet again. The uncharted places are no longer uncharted because you've found them and immersed yourself in them, tamed the dragons, and discovered the magic of your co-creative abilities. Yes, the magic is yours!

PATIENCE AND AWE

There's nothing more breathtaking than seeing the Grand Canyon or other natural rock formations carved out over millennia by flowing water. For all its gentleness and lack of form, water is so strong it can cut rock over time. If you're getting impatient pushing against obstacles in the world of form, and thinking that going with the flow is a sign of weakness, let's get real. Some things in life are the equivalent of having to cut through rock to get to where you want to go, and you need patience. You also need awe, because that gives birth to experiences that are, well, awesome—worthy of your admiration and wonder. Life is a miracle and you get to participate in it.

Yes, we all want certainty and we want to rush Spirit to get all this transformation stuff over with ASAP so we can relax into familiarity again. We all love to linger by the still waters of the resting pond. But if we stay too long, we'll get itchy to move on to another adventure, or Spirit will send a breeze across its surface and we'll sense that it is time to set off on a new journey to uncharted places.

Awe happens when time slows down and you open your heart to the present moment and the beauty of life regardless of outer conditions. Stop, rest, and let gratitude and amazement fill your heart. Awe slows down time so that you can do what you need to do, even when there is a frightening deadline facing you or a big decision you have to make. Awe places you in the Realm of Spirit and reminds you that magic is possible. Miracles happen in front of your eyes daily. They reveal themselves to you when you let yourself stop to feel awe.

When I'm at our farm, where we're tasked to steward the land and the creatures that pass through it, I am clearly and palpably aware of the relationship between Spirit and Form. I know my commitment is to take care of and be the guardian of this place. In honoring that, I receive in return a gift: the deepest sense of peace I have ever had in my life.

When we visited the very first time, I was very much aware of the busyness and mental anxiety I brought with me. I was worrying that we had no phone reception and no Internet, that it was so—well, so much a farm! I'm a city girl, so this felt very new to me. Then I decided to walk around our land and introduce myself to the trees and to the grasses, the flowers, and fields, and to the brook, and even to the insects (of which there are so many!). I thanked everything I looked at. I sent messages of love to all the birds that chirped and chattered, to the crows, and to the eagle that flew overhead (that one I asked to stay away from my tiny dogs). When I was done, I was bursting with love and celebration I don't remember ever having before. I also didn't realize how desperate I had been for this peace and this communion with nature. Spirit called me to this land.

Does it change when I get caught up in the busy schedule, the social media, the touring, writing, and TV-show taping, and the overall velocity of life? Of course! We have all chosen to incarnate into a world of contrasts, and each one of us has a unique purpose that those contrasts help us discover. Deep compassion comes from first experiencing its opposite. Appreciation comes from first experiencing a sense of want. So if you're rushing about and find yourself freaking out now and then, don't feel ashamed. It happens! But contain it. Give yourself 10 minutes of panicking and then sit and reconnect to Spirit. This is the right use of will—choosing to consciously be present in the Divine matrix. I am no different from you. I need to do the same work to stay awake.

When you open to the Realm of Spirit and make a practice of using techniques to turn on your intuitive abilities so you can dialogue with the Divine, you get sign after sign through the Realm of Form that it's all good and Spirit is working with you—so pay attention. Impossible things *are* possible in the Realm of Form. Even so, your job is to remain flexible about what manifests and when.

THE FLEXIBILITY OF FORM

Taking this journey into the uncharted, participating in the co-creative evolutionary process of transforming yourself and therefore your life, makes you realize just how attached you've been to the timing and form of what your small self wants to experience. Now that you've become aware of energy and of the many ways in which you can create something new by directing it well, you can understand why what you manifest won't always look exactly like what you envisioned or show up when you expect. If you were hoping for abundance in the form of enough money to do something you long to do, you might find that abundance takes a different form, and you may come to see that ultimately you got what you truly wanted. I had dreamed of having a television show, and my vision was that it would appear on a big American television network. The show ended up on a smaller Canadian network, but it was so perfect and such a life-changing, marvelous experience, I realized I was actually glad that what I envisioned manifested just as it did.

On the other end of the dreaming and envisioning spectrum, you can get exactly what you want right down to the last detail but find you are disappointed by what you attracted and manifested. This happens when you don't do the work of taking the journey inward to discover what your soul craves and you don't align your small self's will with your soul's longing and the will of Spirit. I always knew I wanted singing and songwriting to be a part of my life—and they have been. But when I was younger, I desperately wanted a record deal and a career in the music business as a singer/songwriter. I pushed and pushed and did all the spiritual work around it—you name it, affirmations, vision boards, creative visualization ad infinitum. Doors slammed in my face. I forgot about "wearing it loosely" and only remained in the desire. Well, do that and all you get is more desire! So I started to do readings, aromatherapy, Reiki, and other work that paid my bills and I gave up on the hope of getting a record deal. Then 10 years passed, and *kaboom*, to the tiniest detail, it all fell into place.

I got just what I wanted—the elusive record deal, with a major label no less. But quickly I realized it wasn't right for me. I was out of place because I was pegged a "mature" artist and dismissed by many in the industry as "over the hill" when I had really just begun! And the career as a singer didn't fit me anymore because I wasn't the same me who started this whole thing going. Who I had become was not the same girl who would have done just about anything to get that deal. Also, I didn't want to concern myself with my looks all the time to keep up with what was (and is) for me an unrealistic beauty standard. And I had become a morning person, so I didn't want to stay up all night or sing in bars (plus, being sober, being in bars was a temptation I didn't need). I recorded my CD, and I got to work with some of the most accomplished and talented musicians in the industry—a dream come true! Yet I knew, I just knew, that this wasn't what I was supposed to be doing. I wasn't willing to do what it took to keep it going. Exhausted by the ambition for the success, I had lost the love of the art along the way.

"Be careful what you wish for" is good advice. Wish carefully—and align your will and intent with the will of Spirit. Then watch the magic unfold before you. The form it takes will be perfect. I'm proud of what I accomplished in that part of my career. Now when I listen to the music I recorded back then, I remember how inspired I was creating it. That's what counts today. So with a new perspective, everything is exactly as it was supposed to be. And I'm back singing, and I love it for the sake of the art alone! Who cares how old I am or how much I weigh? When you let go and let the form take the shape Spirit has in mind, aligned with the intention for the highest good, amazing things happen.

It's in the Realm of Energy, where you're dealing with archetypal energies in the abstract before they take form, that ideas about form should originate—not in your small mind! You might meditate and get an image or a word that could be a metaphor for what you're supposed to experience. What you get could also be very specific. Just be flexible about the route it takes to get there, and don't lose patience and try to force matters to get what you think you want the way you think it's supposed to happen. Now you know to stop yourself, tune in to your intuition, and orient yourself in the Realm of Spirit. Feel the awe—and then laugh, because this place is *fun*!

"BECOME AS LITTLE CHILDREN"

Again and again, you will be called to change on the inside to face challenges on the outside. When life feels very serious, it's hard to understand why Spirit would insist that you should *play*, but you have to do it. It's part of resting. First, it gives you a break from the struggle. Look at how children handle the worst crises. They cry, and then suddenly they're off playing. But also, it's in the playing that you start to connect to Spirit again and immerse yourself in the evolutionary process of creating something new. When you lighten up, you remember the creativity that flowed easily for you when you were a child. Yes, your purpose here on earth is serious, and the suffering can be intense, but you are also supposed to experience joy and laughter. Earnestness can be extremely draining. Lighten up and become like a curious, optimistic, innocent child again—at least for a short while to remind yourself of what life should feel like much of the time. (It's probably not an accident that the Gospel of Matthew calls this the way to the kingdom of heaven!) It will reconnect you to your power to co-create something new. And remember: The Realm of Form responds like a mirror. It will reflect back to you any sustained and repeated state of mind.

Play and laughter will also make it easier to act "as if" and pretend you are ready for what you want to manifest. Play dress-up: Try on the experience for size and see if you like how it feels. Visualize what you'd like to experience and be gentle with yourself when a part of you says, "That could never happen for me," or "I'm not the type of person who could make that happen or be in that situation." If you're feeling pessimistic and foolish for even daring to dream what you're dreaming, that's a sign you're having a moment of disconnection from your soul. You always know when you've unplugged from Spirit as doubt is the domain of the small self, not the soul. You have to go through the process of co-creative evolution and discover who you might be—and play with the possibilities.

See your life as a game because from the perspective of your soul, that's what it is. Co-creating, dancing, and playing with Spirit are what you came to do here in the tangible physical world you experience with your senses. Come and splash in the magical uncharted waters, which are calling you to jump in and discover who you really are.

WHERE SPIRIT AND FORM MEET

The Realm of Form is associated with the physical world, but Spirit is numinous, so Spirit is not just up there in the clouds or over there in a church or on a sacred mountain but here, with you.

Where do you most easily feel Spirit's presence? When you're in a crowd or when you're alone? In a house of worship or a home that has been well loved? Do you feel Spirit in your own home or in other places where you spend much of your time? Are there natural places that feel like sacred spaces to you? Maybe you've been to Sedona or Machu Picchu, or the red rocks in Colorado, or sacred wells in the United Kingdom. Maybe there's a grove of trees in the park near your home that feels like a sacred space. Look for the places that make it easier to remember your interconnectedness, and spend time there. Invite Spirit in. Spirit's already there, but calling Spirit to make its presence known and felt to you helps you remember that there's more to life than what your senses experience in the Realm of Form.

Spirit is everywhere, but it can be very hard to feel it when you are in a place that holds for you memories of an unhappy past. You might even find that you pick up on unhappy memories and uncomfortable energies in places where someone else experienced sadness, anger, or tragedy. You can always call Spirit in to bring in new energies to that place. Then your memories and perception of the place can change.

When Marc and I began to feel called back to Canada after being away for nine years, I knew I had to reclaim some of the places in and around Toronto since we wanted to move to a place near there. Both our families were there, and most of my closest friends were too. Shooting my TV show in the city of my birth should have felt victorious! Yet I had so many unresolved painful memories of this place; I had the feeling every time I visited it that I wasn't finished and couldn't begin again until I stopped running. That was the most difficult thing to admit: that although I had loved our adventure away all those years, I was running the whole time, running from the memories of what had happened to my family, who I had been, who I couldn't be, and who I'd never be.

But it was time to go back and move forward, so I made a conscious choice to deal with the bad memories I'd experienced in Toronto. I had to reclaim the area so that I could live there remembering the past without being held hostage by it.

Author Meggan Watterson once wrote about these places and how they call us: "You know those places that you dread going back to because you don't want to relive what you felt when you were last there . . . the ghost towns that haunt us . . . that we might try to avoid but invariably end up returning to because something in us that's wiser than our fear wants us to make a new memory, wants us to come back for the heart we left there."

I sat down to write an inventory of every unresolved hurt, every instance of unrequited shame, fear, and rage that was part of my story in that city. With purpose, for 40 days, I worked my way through every realm. All was revealed in bits and pieces, shards and strips, and I released myself from the stories that belonged to me but were no longer meant to remain with me as I journeyed inward to a new me, free of those constrictions. My past self needed to sleep, for she was tired and had suffered so much. I could take her wisdom and leave her forgiveness as a gift, but it was time to leave her behind.

The results were only internal at first, and then they started showing up in my reactions to things, in first impressions, and even in the way I walked down the street. I maintained a sense of curiosity, noticing that the places that once haunted me had no more ghosts to talk to. But then an opportunity presented itself to me in the Realm of Form.

When Marc and I first arrived in Toronto, we spent time in an expensive hotel in a very swank area of the city that held many of my most shameful memories—experiences I rarely think about unless I'm physically there. I walked around the area and was amazed that I found myself completely neutral and detached. The buildings had no "charge" for me, no echoes to taunt me, just compassion for the young girl that was me back then. Elated, I decided to celebrate, and so I walked over to a store where I knew I could buy some organic berries and my favorite eucalyptus bubble bath.

I walked in and saw a man a short distance away. I immediately recognized him. He was one of the most handsome men around "back in the day," a man with a reputation as long and venomous as a snake, and I was one of the many women who stood beside him at a bar and was offered a drink with a secret in it. There was confusion and shame—and I was quickly discarded. In the past, seeing him would cause my palms to sweat in fear as he would always try to remind me of how I didn't fight. "You must have wanted it."

Here we were, 35 years later.

There he was, someone whose memory had held all my power, my dignity, and my self-worth as motionless as a bug in amber. But now I saw him with clarity: an aging man trying to be cool, alone and trying to hang on to something he might never have had. I felt a wave of compassion flow through me. He recognized me, but I saw how he was struggling to put it all together. He swaggered over, smiling yet shaking, pushing his thinning hair back through his fingers. "How are you?" he said. "Wow! You look so amazing. You look different, but the same—like you have never changed! But now you just glow."

I just smiled, and to my surprise, I was calm as could be. The memories were neutral, and I replied, "Thanks; I'm doing great. I'm just not her anymore."

And I meant it.

Walking home, I pondered what had happened.

When we reclaim a place, we "come back for the heart we left there." And in so doing, we love the ghosts away, we retrieve our self-worth and the truth we were too afraid to face, and the Realm of Form begins to reflect a new vision of reality.

RECLAIMING A SPACE

If you have been traumatized in a space, or if you have a story about a place that brings up energy and emotion within you that causes you to relive the pain, you can change the memories of it that live within you and alter the energy of the locale to be more peaceful and loving. Places hold memories just like people do, and you can affect that. And when you change the energy of the place, it will be like a ripple effect, as even the people associated with the events that took place there will no longer trigger you either.

One of my coaching clients did the following Reclaiming the Space exercise before he visited his hometown, where he had been the victim of bullying in high school because he was gay. He told me that whenever he went to visit his family on holidays, he had to drive past the school, and he always cringed. After doing the exercise at home, he visited his parents and found he felt no emotional charge when he passed the school, so he decided to do the ritual again—this time on-site. He said it felt as if an invisible weight was lifted off his back, and he could see the place through a different lens. He saw himself as he truly was, and he was able to set that former self free, as well as to set the walls of the building, his homeroom, and even his locker free.

Six months later, he accepted an invitation to his high school reunion. Not only did he have a wonderful time seeing some of his old friends, but the bully himself was there too and came right over to apologize for his behavior! My client now has new memories and a new association with this place that brings him peace and hope instead of anxiety and shame.

The purpose of this exercise is to know how essence is the basis for form. Change the essence, and the meaning associated with the form changes; then the form has a different use or application, and your experience with that form will change too.

Exercise: Reclaiming the Space

You can do this exercise for changing the energy of a space where you were hurt, either by using your imagination or by going to the actual space. Be sure you have some privacy, and have a pen and paper or a journal ready so that you can write about your experience of this exercise either during it or afterward.

Take a few deep breaths and allow your mind to slow down in meditation. Let your body relax. Draw your attention first to your breathing and then to how you feel in this place.

What comes up for you emotionally?

What do you remember about this place and the things that happened here?

What meaning have you applied to the events of this place?

Now imagine the place has an ancient residing Spirit that lives there and knows the stories of the events that have taken place there. Imagine you are approaching this place as you are now, today, and you greet the residing Spirit, who is holding a beautiful box. This box contains the essence of your memories of this place. This Spirit has been holding it for you until you were ready for this moment. Now you are going to change the quality of your memories by bringing new energy to them.

Imagine that the Spirit waves a hand in the air and a table and two chairs appear in front of you. The two chairs are facing each other. One chair is empty, and in the other sits your past self—the you who experienced the original event. Sit opposite this past self.

You're meant to go through the box of memories with this past self to help yourself see who you were and who you have become. You're there to offer love and compassion and support and to set your past self free so the form of the place can take on a new energy and a new meaning.

Hold the box in your hands and peer into it. You will see a stack of memories, like postcards or snapshots. Take one out and talk to your old self about it. Tell your old self, "This is what happened then, but because that happened, something very good happened too." Tell your old self about the wisdom you acquired or the qualities you developed that made you a better person or helped you better understand yourself.

Express love to your past self. Watch as the postcard turns into a sparkling butterfly that floats away from your hand up into the sky. As it goes, pay attention to how you feel and how the energy surrounding your past self changes too.

Continue to go through the postcard memories in this way, expressing love to your past self, explaining how each memory led to something good, then watching it turn into a butterfly and fly away. When you are finished, look at your past self and express love.

Who could this past self become now within you?

Notice how the Spirit of the place changes, and how the place itself changes. Notice what you perceive.

When you feel complete, imagine the Spirit of the place takes a ball of pure light and energy and places it on your head as a blessing and a benediction—and then does the same for your past self. Embrace your past self and let it know how much you love it.

Say the following words over and over until you are ready to open your eyes and end the exercise: *Spirit is everywhere. Only Love is real.*

SPIRIT'S PRESENCE IN EVERYDAY LIFE

We want to feel Spirit in our everyday lives. I'm not Catholic, but I love Pope Francis, who has done an extraordinary job reminding people of aspects of Christianity and Catholicism that have been overlooked too often—like service to the poor and rejection of materialism. He was quoted as saying he wished he could spend more time among everyday people, just having pizza with them. Isn't that what we want on our end—a chance to have a pizza and relax with Spirit? I don't want to feel that God is far away, reachable only through prayer and never able to communicate directly with me. I want Spirit to make its presence known on the bus, in the airport, and at the restaurant.

We associate the physical world with things that aren't of Spirit, but it's all part of the matrix, and the Great Mind is active everywhere. There is no separation between Spirit and the mundane (which comes from a Latin word meaning "the world"). We just have to tune in to remind ourselves that Spirit is here, alongside us, with us, in us, and everywhere. We talk ourselves out of believing this, though, because we don't want to seem naïve or foolish about this "miracle" stuff. There is a lot of pressure to buy into a worldview of scientific materialism, the belief that everything "out there" is mechanistic and without soul or consciousness. Quantum physics has shown us that the world is not a simple machine with parts that move predictably, but we still cling to that idea instead of recognizing that Spirit exists in the places in between—in the invisible realms we think are empty. Spirit is the ghost in the machine that we can't see with human eyes, but we can open up to the evidence of its presence. We see the footprints of Spirit, the patterns that show the Great Mind is online and present, affecting our lives.

Darwin looked at the everyday, natural world and saw a pattern: competition and what others later dubbed "survival of the fittest." What he missed was what lay beneath that competition that was visible in the Realm of Form: He missed the collaboration. That's the pattern of Spirit! If not for the rabbit giving itself up to the hawk, the hawk couldn't play the game. It wouldn't survive. What looks cruel to us is just life expressing itself in a collaborative dance. The everyday world exists alongside the hidden matrix in which everything is interconnected in an energy grid and patterns of interconnectedness.

Even in the perceived cruelty of nature, we recognize the majesty and the dance of perfection. Many of us feel closer to Spirit in nature because we're reminded of this cycle of life and the inherent beauty of it. Nature is always adjusting to maintain balance. The more we live in man-made spaces lit by man-made lights, communicating on man-made technological devices, the more important it is to remember to reconnect with Spirit through nature.

WHEN'S THE LAST TIME YOU CHECKED IN WITH YOUR MOTHER—MOTHER NATURE?

A lot of us have neglected our relationship to our environment—the planet itself and the people and creatures around us. Everything is supposed to be in balance and constantly evolving. That means some species die and some are born, and we participate in this co-creative, evolutionary process. We can do this without giving up our desire to survive as a species in the Realm of Form because life here on earth is what we intend to experience—for now. We don't have to run off and start planning a move to colonies on Mars, although that may be next. But we do have to engage in a co-creative, collaborative, evolutionary process here on earth. Let's allow our imaginations to explore possibilities and remember how to play like children, picturing in our minds what we can do, even though saving the planet and ourselves is serious business. Solutions are being discovered every day. Remember it takes time for the Realm of Form to catch up. You and I are looking at the conditions of our world set in motion by the minds and actions of the past. Many of us have evolved past them, which is why there is so much dissonance and uncertainty. What form will we create to replace the conditions in front of us so we can live harmoniously and sustainably on this planet and she can continue to support us? We need to go beyond what we see now. We need to trust that in the uncharted is where the new world can be created. Our task is to journey there.

I know many of you are bogged down in the challenges of your everyday life. I get it. The other day when I was trying to write, it was 97 degrees and my air-conditioning wasn't working, and I was completely distracted. As they say, "first world problem." I am grateful that air-conditioning exists and that it's not 108 degrees in the shade! But the body that belongs to Colette Baron-Reid wanted some relief right then and there. That's okay—there's no shame in desiring comfort and relief from challenges in the Realm of Form. But at the same time, I was aware that the unusual weather patterns are ones we co-created because of choices we made in the past—and we have to start making some different ones so we can all live sustainably on the earth. Having that dual awareness of what each of us as individuals wants and needs and what we all want and need as members of the human race is required of as many people as possible right now. And having an awareness of our relationship to the planet matters more than ever.

All ancient spiritual traditions that still influence us today say that God or the many gods created the heavens and the earth. No matter whether we think of it as the One or the many in the One, we have sensed this great truth since we first walked the earth. Because we're a part of Spirit, we were a part of that creative endeavor. The earth is our home, and like us, it has consciousness and participates in the great collective consciousness of the matrix, called Spirit. Every indigenous culture has a creation myth that incorporates the idea that the earth has awareness—something that has more recently been called Gaia theory.

We communicate with the consciousness of the earth in many ways. One way is through microbes. We actually have more of these little microscopic organisms in our bodies than we have cells that belong to us and have our DNA. These organisms live in us and on us, so our cells are dialoguing with them in ways scientists are just beginning to discover. Just in the last few years, researchers have come to recognize that the microbes that line our gut form our immune system and play a huge role in the biochemistry of our brain and the moods we experience. Did you know that a colony of intestinal microbes that lacks diversity can cause depression and muddled thinking and even lead to disease processes? Did you know that altering your microbiome in your gut by bringing in new microorganisms can reverse these problems? Although we're just learning about the mechanisms, clearly there's a conversation going on between us and the creatures outside of us that live on the earth, in the trees, and in the air that we breathe—for those places are where the microbes originate. Gardening and touching the earth actually replenishes healthy colonies of microbes in your gut. Think about that. We're supposed to be touching the earth and bringing her into us to live in a symbiotic relationship.

Here's another partnership we have with the planet we live on and are a part of: We inhale life-giving oxygen and exhale carbon dioxide that the plants inhale, and they in turn exhale oxygen. It's perfect teamwork!

What can we do for the earth to make sure that she can continue to help us? Let's talk to her and find out. Spend time in nature, paying attention to how the earth speaks to you and reminds you of the interconnectedness of life. Respond to her messages and thank her for supporting you. Feel grateful for the earth beneath your feet.

Our ancestors, who didn't have the technologies we have developed in the last few hundred years, understood this connection with the earth. Some forgot their connections before others did, and the loss of connection for many societies came about gradually. We crawled into our heads and forgot we'd once crawled out of the ocean and onto the earth. We developed scientific ideas and more sophisticated technologies, and we used the lamplight to read more, think more, and do more. We started to see the planet as something to subdue and conquer, a resource to feed our new ways of operating. Planning where to put our waste, imagining what we were going to do if we killed a river or caused a species to become extinct—we weren't doing any of that. Fortunately, we're now beginning to wake up to how much we have disrespected our home.

So how does this relate to you in the Realm of Form? For one thing, you can choose to stop living in your head so much and start spending more time sitting under a tree or on the ground, feeling the grass, sand, or earth beneath you. It will help you to remember your nature as a human being on the planet Earth.

Our bodies can't survive without the earth and the food, air, and water she provides. We know this intellectually, and we can pay lip service to it, but we haven't internalized in our bones that this is the time for radical evolution of the human experience and a revolution in our relationship with the earth.

But ah, you now know how to write a new story, don't you? You know how to participate in the co-creative evolutionary process. The Realm of Form is not going to kick you or any of us out of it, because every day, more of us are waking up and joining in the collaboration to save ourselves and the planet. Recently, I've read about some young women who discovered a microbe that eats plastic and converts it to organic matter, and a new effort to gather the plastic in the ocean and clean it up. We're learning that highly effective solar panels can be made even smaller and more efficient. Iceland's energy sources are 100 percent renewable. We should be excited to be a part of this incredible evolution!

Everything we are experiencing we helped co-create. It started in consciousness and worked its way into manifesting in form. Let's connect with the Realm of Spirit, using our intuition, and keep aligning our personal consciousness with the consciousness of Spirit. The answers will flow through, the ideas will come, and we can creatively collaborate like crazy.

I know it can be hard to resist the cynicism that says we come from form, we live in form, and we'd better work hard to battle each other and the elements of the earth in order to survive in form. We'd better get those oceans to stop sending us hurricanes and protect ourselves from flooding. Yes, we should do what we need to do in the Realm of Form, but we'll have a much better idea of what to do if we start as always in the Realm of Spirit, orienting ourselves there before trying to fix our problems. You are here, I am here, we are here. We can work together.

Still feeling skeptical? That's okay. Just don't be cynical.

Consciousness is the untapped resource that we've been overlooking. The age of agriculture gave way to the age of industry, which gave way to the age of information—and next will come the age of consciousness, which makes sense. After all, what good is information if you don't use it consciously and wisely?

Look into the world and you see chaos, and it's scary. Uncertainty is everywhere. You can't find lasting security in any home, job, or relationship, because everything transforms and things fall away. Of course, that has always been true, but we are experiencing it more than ever, so uncertainty is very much on our minds. Whatever we have created, we have to remember that these forms—how we "do" work, play, school, relationships—were set in motion by our old selves, by the thoughts and actions of a past culture. Our attention now must be on a reality that is not visible yet. We all need to step into the void, where the new ideas are waiting for us to claim them, not go back to the "way things were."

If you do what you did, you'll get what you got.

We're at the tipping point, and we need to take the leap of faith and step into being co-creators. The leap of faith takes us from the Realm of Form into the Realm of Spirit, and into the spiraling journey through the realms of co-creation so we can evolve into new selves ready for the new world we've helped birth into being. The world we need to co-create is very different from the one we'll be forced to leave behind.

I'm not one for waiting, are you? So let's work together and manifest something new in the world of form. Let's see the temporary conditions as they are—the product of the thinking of our past selves. Let's calibrate our souls and small selves and trust that in the invisible is everything we need. The uncharted part of the Map is where we must go. It is calling to us to co-create something better—for ourselves and for each other.

Traveler's Notes

- In the Realm of Form, co-creation happens as you immerse yourself in the flow of the Divine with feet firmly planted on the ground. Life becomes easier because you notice you have a manifesting partner in Spirit.
- The universe is starting to reflect your new story and your higher vibration. It is catching up to where you are inside.
- You now realize that your soul's ideas about what to co-create, which are informed by Spirit, were far wiser than your small self's ideas.

- Having taken the journey, you make better decisions and feel more clarity and joy and lightness of being.
- Now, whenever spiritual narcolepsy kicks in, you will be asleep to your spiritual nature for a much shorter period, and with self-compassion, you'll easily return to an integrated state.
- Because you have done the work of self-evolution, you feel comfortable in your own skin and in the life you have chosen for yourself. You receive signs that Spirit is continuing to work through you to make the seemingly impossible possible.
- If you get what you want, even right down to the last detail, but find you are disappointed by what you attracted and manifested, it is because you skipped the work of the journey through the five interconnected realms.
- Spirit is numinous, but some places feel exceptionally sacred and some bear painful memories. Visit sacred spaces and reclaim any spaces where you have bad memories by transforming the energy there. Love the ghosts away so the spaces or the people associated with them no longer have a charge for you.
- Remember that while there is competition in the everyday, natural world, underneath it is connection and collaboration.
- Communicate with the consciousness of the earth through gardening, touching the earth, spending time with her, breathing in an exchange with plants—and not living in your head so much.
- Banish fear by remembering that the forms you see before you were set in motion by our old selves, and new forms are already being co-created by you and others.
- In the Realm of Form, rest at times, play at others, and dance when you can. Enjoy the game and lighten up like you're supposed to do.

11

OFF YOU GO!

Every one of us chose to participate in this grand adventure of life on earth, to take form in bodies whose senses would distract us from our spiritual nature. It's an adventure! Let's enjoy it!

But be forewarned: No matter how much we value spirituality, think of ourselves as spiritual, or engage in spiritual practices, we all have to accept that spiritual narcolepsy is an unavoidable condition of living in a body. We can control it, but we can never cure it completely.

It's true. I didn't offer you a magic fix, after all. Magic, yes. But no one can rescue you from the problems inherent in the complex, unpredictable, exquisitely frustrating but always amusing experience called being human.

I'll be honest: Your small self is going to nod off now and again and forget your soul's purpose. So is mine. It will even forget that your soul exists. You are going to realize at times that, oops, you fell asleep and really screwed up. We all do. We start taking life too seriously, forget about the Realm of Spirit and our spiritual nature, and then the dragons take off, flying about and setting all sorts of things on fire. We misuse our personal power and people get hurt—including us.

Your small self might be able to see there's a problem, that the old behavior patterns you swore off have somehow cropped up again. But even if your small self does have an inkling of what's going on, it is likely to remain in denial and insist, "It's okay! I can fix this!" Then you'll continue to hurt others and be hurt in return.

Your outer conditions will reflect the shame, anger, and fear inside you—the feelings you have because you know you are making a mess of things.

But the good news is now that you have begun doing the work of this book, you'll slip back into the old ways less often. You will awaken more quickly to what is going on and what role you play in it. You'll take ownership of those dragons and their destructiveness and get back to using your power wisely. Uncertainty won't discombobulate you and make you want to run, because you will know that the uncharted places are where the magic happens—and you can help make it happen. You'll find the courage to take risks and be creative, along with the patience to be gentle with yourself as you venture forth.

The other good news is that your soul self, your authentic nature, will be expressed more and more, helping you to feel you are living according to your purpose—because you are! Instead of getting in your way, your small self will be aligning with your soul self and working with it instead of against it. The magic will work when you are not looking—when you aren't forcing matters. Perseverance is good. Banging your head against a wall, saying, "This must change now!"—not so much.

To make magic happen, you have to actually commit to *integrating* the ideas you have read about in this book. Start thinking about what spiritual practices you would like to try out and which you would like to use more often. What can you do to make the ideas in this book real for you? As I wrote earlier, "Your gas tank doesn't get filled just because you know where the gas station is!" Don't put this book down and say, "That was nice. Gotta remember all that." You know what can happen . . . Zzzzzz! So make a commitment to experiencing and expressing your authenticity, to opening conversations with Spirit and listening and watching for Spirit's response. Commit to opening your heart to the vastness of Spirit's potential for co-creation. You have the most awe-inspiring collaborative partner possible, so check in and check your small self's tendency to think, *I can do this all by myself.* Your small self can be like a toddler—cute, yearning for independence and self-expression, but in need of a lot of guidance and redirection.

Regular spiritual practice looks different for everyone. As I said, I meditate twice a day, use oracles, and spend time walking around my farm and listening to the chirping and chattering of the birds, tuning in to the messages from Spirit. Your practice might involve prayer, journaling, yoga—there are so many possibilities. If you are struggling to find what works to help you stay connected, make some changes to your everyday life, including during those times of the day when you are most aware of moving into a different state of consciousness: when you are first waking up in the morning and when you are going to sleep at night.

MORNING, NOON, AND NIGHT, YOU CAN RECONNECT

When you awaken in the morning, before you do anything else, pause to remember this incredible gift you have just been given: You get to co-create with Spirit for another day. Consciously set the intention to bring forth something beautiful and meaningful. Say a prayer of gratitude. Ask Spirit to help you to stay awake to your soul and its calling. Think about what you want to experience and who you want to become.

How will you shine today? Imagine that before you lay your head on your pillow again at the end of the day, your light will join the light of others and the world will be a better place in some way, however small. What will that look like?

Keep in mind what Elizabeth Gilbert said in her book *Big Magic*: "You're not required to save the world with your creativity." Telling a good joke, holding someone's hand for a few moments to connect with them in love—sometimes that is what really matters. It's your small self that thinks you have to make a big splash to have any impact. Don't cramp your brain with anxiety about all that you might do. Be present. Breathe. Set your intention for the day. That's enough. You are enough.

At night, before you fall asleep, check in with yourself and Spirit. Write in a journal, meditate, pray, or simply look out the window as you introspect and listen for messages from Spirit that show up in sparkling snow, the random appearance of a dog walker on your street, or a cloud kissing the face of the moon. How did you do today? Did spiritual narcolepsy kick in or did you feel your soul self and Spirit at hand, present and guiding you? If you did nod off and do something dumb, can you forgive yourself for being imperfect and making mistakes? Can you practice radical self-acceptance and laugh at your little screwups? Can you lighten up and let go of the heaviness of your day?

And if you feel you did significant harm—maybe you said something awful to someone because you were angry or scared—remember, you can ask for forgiveness. Love yourself enough to forgive yourself, to radically accept yourself in all your beautiful, messy imperfection. Learn from what happened, and ask Spirit to help you do better tomorrow—and find the words and actions that will bring light and love to the situation you set in motion. Think about how you can do better tomorrow and be better tomorrow. Say a prayer of gratitude because life is good and you are here.

Each day, be vigilant without being anxious. Look for any signs that you nodded off; gave in to your ego's desire to play it safe; and avoided taking big, creative risks that both your small self and your soul self know you need to take. When you recognize you wanted to speak your truth, in love, to another person, but backed away in fear of "making waves"—yep, you nodded off. When you realize you walked away from an opportunity to discover a part of yourself you secretly hope is within you, because you know you need to bring that into the light—you nodded off. When you took the easy path instead of the more challenging one, only to find yourself on the back roads, feeling victimized, lost, and frustrated—uh-huh, you did it again.

Stay present in the moment, surrendering to what is. Observe it. Don't get ahead of yourself. Be here, in the now, today, instead of focused on what might happen tomorrow or what should have happened yesterday. Remember, when your awareness is focused on the past or the future instead of the now, you can end up stuck in Ghostlands where your mind is in overdrive with all its pointless, fruitless ruminations. In Ghostlands, you are powerless to effect change because everything is happening in your head—catastrophes, conflicts, and a cascade of problems that overwhelm you. You can't fix any of them until you come back to the present moment and remember you are connected to a vast consciousness whose wisdom, power, and love are always there for you.

You can trust your intuition and "phone home" to Spirit at any time to have a conversation and feel connected to infinite possibility. Remain present and become the observer. Use the exercises to awaken your power to step back from the feeling of being overwhelmed and to survey what you are experiencing and how you might interact with your situation differently.

And claim your personal power—train your dragons! Stop feeding them junk food. Don't be afraid to use your power to express yourself and make changes in your life. You can trust yourself. Even if you end up on back roads, you will either enjoy the scenic route or consciously return to the road you wanted to be on. Either way, you will have the experience your soul yearned to have, so it's all good.

LIVING AUTHENTICALLY

In the movie *Adaptation,* there's a wonderful line: "You are what you love, not what loves you." That's what authenticity is all about. Free yourself of all the burdens of attachment, including your attachment to external approval. It's only natural to want to see an outward reflection of your "okayness." But when you're seeking that, you are not in your power.

You are in your power when you choose what you love instead of choosing what loves you. Being creative is your soul's way of expressing itself, through your small self, through any number of situations that you might co-create that show up for you in the Realm of Form. I know I am most alive when I'm allowing my individuality to simply be and letting creativity run through me. I feel energized by this gift from Spirit, the Source of all creation. When I surrender to the flow of Spirit's loving, creative energy, when I let myself be me, I feel the greatest sense of belonging. I don't feel I have to conform to someone's expectations of what I am supposed to be. I just *am.*

How much of what you do, how you interact with others, is rooted in conformity? What did you agree to without protest because you felt it would be easier to submit to what was happening around you—the goings-on in an upside-down world that values money more than people and power more than bliss? What is your truth? That's the question you have to ask yourself again and again. Slow down enough to question what is and who you are. Take a breath, close your eyes, and enter the Realm of Spirit. You are here. What do you want to experience? What does your soul need to express? What do you want to create? Creating security on earth is not the primary goal. Co-creating something new that reflects the best of who you are and who you can become—that is the goal.

Open to the possibility of creating something even better, something more. Do this even if you have experienced success. Why cling to what you created and think you can't expand on it? That's just not true. Begin the co-creative process and let your heart open to all the ways in which your intentions can express themselves in the Realm of Form.

Go ahead and let your small self brew up a few ideas, but don't leave it at that. Engage in the co-creative process that begins in the Realm of Spirit and you will be so much more satisfied than if you simply worked in the Realm of Form trying to manifest as best you can. If you do what you did, you're going to get what you got. Take the journey through the five interconnected realms to do, and get, something new. And whatever you end up deciding you would like to manifest—you are going to have some ideas, after all—tell yourself, "This or something better."

WHERE ARE YOU GOING?

The uncharted beckons. You are called to transformation. That requires you to enter the cocoon or chrysalis and trust in a process of evolution that will turn you into the person you need to be to live the life you want to live. When you emerge, you will blink, flap your new wings in preparation for flight, and see that the old you is still there, along with all your memories, but they have been integrated into this new you who is ready for the next adventure.

And your Map? The lines of silvery light will sparkle as you see connections between the familiar places, pathways you overlooked before. The heartaches, the "wrong" turns—it all makes so much more sense now. Ahhh. It is easier to trust in this process now!

So what's next? Off you go—to participate in the co-creation of a new world. Your evolution has been more important than you realize. According to quantum physics, there's something called the butterfly effect: seemingly small, random events affect our shared field of energy in such a way that, theoretically, the flapping of a butterfly's wings could cause a storm to brew on the other side of the world.

It is okay not to know just where you are, what you are doing, or where you need to go. That experience of not knowing is temporary. With you and Spirit working together in love, the Map will get filled in exactly as it is supposed to. Everything will come together, arranging itself through the power of love and the guidance of our shared consciousness. You'll know what you need to know when you need to know it.

ALL TOGETHER NOW!

The multidimensional Maps of our souls intersect each other in a complex interplay. Nothing is separate unless you choose to see it that way—and if you do, you can set up conflicts that prevent healing. It's easy to see people whose beliefs and actions don't seem in sync with yours as different from you, and to see the difference as a problem, but guess what? They are a part of your life. You can't avoid them completely. To "love your enemy" is hard, but it's completely necessary. And remember this—they are *not* your enemy. They are your *mirror.* They are here to remind you to look within and pay attention to what you are co-creating and what you co-created in the past that is taking shape in the Realm of Form now.

When you most feel cynical and want to march out and hurt someone else who is harming others, that's when you most need to bring peace into your own heart. Fortunately, Spirit is always there to help soothe you—and Spirit often works through other people, and animals and nature too. Reconnect! Love begets love. However upset you get, remember the power of love to help all of us heal and evolve.

Whatever your individual challenges, they will be less daunting when you join the tribe of people working together to raise our consciousness. Together, we are evolving into the people we need to be to have the experiences of peace, harmony, and prosperity on earth with its seven billion people. How do you join in? By letting the creative, loving force arise in you and flow through you. By being the you that only you can be.

As we enter the age of consciousness, we don't have to convince everyone to see what we're seeing and do what we're doing. We just need enough people courageously venturing within, doing their own work and inspiring others at the same time, to create a tipping point so we can move into the next stage of our human experience. Science and technology will be incredible tools for reversing the damage we've done to the planet and to our bodies, but they are not going to be enough. Transformation in the Realm of Form has to start with a transformation of consciousness. There's a lot of important work to do in the five interconnected realms so that we can manifest a new world. Doing that work is the way we'll fulfill the responsibility that the Chorus Known as Fred showed me: we're here to defend our garden!

The magic now is in marrying our personal journeys of self-evolution with the larger journey of humankind as we co-evolve the consciousness we all share. As we do so, we can all connect to the wonderful, regenerative, and nourishing powers of the earth and all the people who are participating in this co-creation and co-evolution. We're all in the same tribe. Remember what Fred said: *We are We—You are We!* We are unified in the most extraordinary ways. Let's choose joy, have fun, and be present, authentic, and available to each other, expressing love, forgiveness, and creativity as we explore the magical world of the uncharted.

Infinite possibilities are waiting to be discovered.

Ready?

Excellent.

Traveler's Notes

- Spiritual narcolepsy is incurable but manageable if you use spiritual practices to reopen the channels of communication with Spirit.
- Regular spiritual practice looks different for everyone. "Phone home" to Spirit as you come into consciousness in the morning, as you move into dreamland at night, and throughout the day at any time.
- Don't be afraid to use your power to express yourself and make changes in your life. You can trust yourself because your small self is no longer dominating you.
- Co-create something new that reflects the best of who you are and who you can become. Remember that if you do what you did, you're going to get what you got.
- To "love your enemy" is hard, but it's completely necessary. Understand that your "enemy" is not separate from you but a mirror reflecting back to you what you need to transform in yourself.
- Miracles are invoked and called into form, not forced. We are called to co-create magic: to self-evolve and, as a result, help everyone evolve.
- It's time to step joyfully into the magical world of the uncharted. Infinite possibilities are waiting for you!

GLOSSARY

co-creation: When we are in alignment with Spirit, we are aware that we are essentially two parts—human and Spirit combined. Co-creation is deliberately acting as part of a creative partnership with Spirit.

Imagine Spirit has dreamed us, then manifests as a spark of Spirit within us, animating us; when we are inspired through that spark, then we can dream the world. We co-create reality in partnership with Spirit. Our human personalities and our spiritual natures—ego and soul—work together to bring events, things, and intentions into our reality. In a way, we are the paintbrush for Spirit, and at the same time we are the artist creating on the canvas of our lives.

dragons: A metaphor for personal power.

first sense: The sense of intuition.

Though it's often called "the sixth sense," I refer to intuition as the *first* sense as it is the navigational sense of the soul. Since the soul exists before the personality, and I refer to the Realm of Spirit as the primary reality, then intuition cannot be the sixth sense—it has to be the first.

Fred: A group of voices that hum and speak in a singsong-like harmony. They are not human—never have been—and they exist as a resource to help humanity. (At least that's what they said they were doing here!)

They showed up for me as guides at the end of taping my Canadian TV show, *Messages from Spirit*. They talk to me only when I choose to tune in and listen to them. They are still there, and I am not crazy!

Map: The Map of your life, also called the Map of your soul. Through my Mapmaking process (discussed in depth in my book *The Map*), metaphor is used as a tool for self-discovery.

Inside all of us are psychological landscapes created by our thoughts, feelings, beliefs, memories, and intentions. These psycho-spiritual places make up the territories on our Maps, such as the Storm Fields and the Barren Desert. The Map is a journey of self-discovery where can find our own oracles and wisdom within our personal inner landscapes. No two souls' Maps are the same, even if the territories and landscapes are, because no one experiences events in exactly the same way.

Realm of Spirit: The Realm of Spirit is the primary reality. Spirit is the Source of all Life: all ideas, all concepts, all potentials and possibilities come together here in this invisible Consciousness, without exception. The Realm of Spirit refers to the state of formlessness where everything, every form, is possible. It has sometimes been referred to as the "quintessence," where ideas exist in their purest essence before they come into form.

Everything exists in the Realm of Spirit first before it takes form, called into form by our desires, intentions, beliefs, and conditioning. First we are formless, then we take form—all within the vastness of Spirit. It's like invisible cloud storage for every idea that has ever come up from humans or from Spirit, as well as those we have not yet come up with. We can "download" anything once we connect to its essence.

small self: The ego or persona that is necessary to define a person's subjective reality. It is essential as a tool for the unique expression of Spirit. The small self, built and shaped by memory and experience, refers to the self-awareness of the human being. It believes it is separate from the soul and from everything it encounters. It references itself as "me."

Spirit. I use the term *Spirit* to represent the Consciousness of the Universe. It's like saying Divine Intelligence. Spirit is like a matrix where all possibilities exist in essence prior to being brought into form. This intelligence is greater than you and I and is the Source of everything.

Spirit is pure creativity, and it is constantly in motion, dreaming and making, unmaking and evolving. Although, as I mentioned before, I like to stay away from religious connotations, Spirit is synonymous with God. That said, Spirit is not a deity that looks like an old white man in the sky. It can't be contained, nor can it be described in human terms.

Spirit also represents the vastness of this Consciousness. Interchangeably, I use other names you might be familiar with: Great Mind, Source, The Field, The Quantum Field, Cosmic Consciousness, The Universe, Higher Power, The I Am, and so on.

Every one of us, in fact every single life-form, is intrinsically part of Spirit because our life force is part of Spirit and returns to Spirit as Source. So we are unified within Spirit, as immortal spiritual beings having a limited mortal human experience.

spiritual amnesia: This is the state of forgetting that we are spiritual beings and thinking that life is created by self-will alone. Forgetting our purpose and only seeing through the limited lens of scientific materialism. The state of accepted awareness that reality is finite and limited to be experienced and perceived through the five senses.

As souls incarnating, and perhaps even as children, we know that we are spiritual beings. But somewhere along the way, we forget this important truth. Someone in a state of spiritual amnesia has forgotten there is a Higher Power, a Divine Intelligence, that we can tap into to co-create reality. When in spiritual amnesia, we think that this life is the only one and that there is human potential but no spiritual aspect to our existence.

spiritual narcolepsy: This is what happens when you "fall asleep at the wheel" of your life. You temporarily fall prey to fear or subconscious triggers that cause you to forget that you have a co-creative partnership with Spirit, that you are in fact a part of Spirit. You forget that the material world is not the primary reality and start to look at outer conditions as a way to orient yourself instead of tuning within to get where you're at.

This happens when a big change is about to occur and when you're called out of your comfort zone. It's as if you are caught in one part of the cycle of ebb and flow and see only the ebb as the true reality, based on scarcity and limitations. It happens to everybody who believes they are spiritually aware. It's just part of the human condition. We fall asleep once in a while and let our fears take the wheel.

Total Mindshift Process: The name for a trademarked energy psychology technique (previously named the Invision Process) I developed to retrain the subconscious. Elements of the technique were inspired by ancient wisdom traditions and practices, including Carl Jung's active imagination, mindfulness meditation, eco-psychology, voice dialogue, and shamanic journeying. All the exercises in this book are based on this process.

uncharted: A place for which no Map has yet been drawn because the place has not yet been discovered.

The uncharted refers to new experiences that are not based on what you know already. You do not know these places within you yet, nor have you seen evidence of them in the outer world, but you know the adventure is calling you. *Uncharted* implies new experiences waiting to be discovered and known. In the uncharted territories of life lies infinite potential.

READING GROUP GUIDE

You're in the Right Place shows us how to draw our own Map for a journey of discovery—a journey along new paths, to a life full of possibility. You can use these questions as starting points to discuss the guidance Colette offers and explore your own experience.

Colette writes at length about the "old story" we tell ourselves about who we are—and letting go of this story. What is your "old story"?

Describe a time in your life when change felt scary. Can you write a new story describing that change as fun and exciting?

In the book, Fred uses the vast ocean to explain the illusion of separateness and how interconnected we really are. Does this metaphor resonate with you? Why or why not? Are there other forces in nature that help demonstrate this idea?

Colette says that the soul yearns to co-create in community with others. Brainstorm projects that your group can collaborate on.

Consider the importance of gratitude, compassion, and self-acceptance in navigating the uncharted. How have these qualities shaped your own journey?

"Tragedies and traumas are not blessings, but blessings can come out of them." Share some of the blessings in disguise that you have experienced firsthand.

What unexplored places and experiences are calling you right now?

ACKNOWLEDGMENTS

It takes a village to support the birth of a book!

I'd like to thank first and foremost my husband, Marc, who had to put up with me while writing this book. I love you so much.

A special thank you to Reid Tracy. I'm grateful to be home.

Thank you to my awesome editor, Nancy Peske, and to Anne Barthel and Nicolette Salamanca Young—yay team!

Many thanks to these amazing people who have enriched my journey beyond measure (in no particular order): Patty Gift, Andy McNicol, Jennifer Rudolf Walsh, Nancy Levin, John Holland, Jill Buffington, Lisa Toste, Althea Gray, Evelyn Baron, Margarete Nielsen, and all the staff at Hay House.

Last but not least, I'd like to thank Fred!

ABOUT THE AUTHOR

Colette Baron-Reid is an internationally respected author, educator, spiritual intuitive, medium, and oracle expert. Her best-selling books and oracle cards are published worldwide in 27 languages. She is the founder of Oracle School, a global online learning platform with students in 35 countries, where self-empowerment, co-creation, and ancient oracles meet in a modern, contemporary way. Colette is also the creator of the energy psychology technique Invision—The Total Mindshift Process. She divides her time between Canada and the United States with her husband and three funny little Pomeranians.

Visit her at **colettebaronreid.com**.

Hay House Titles of Related Interest

YOU CAN HEAL YOUR LIFE, the movie,
starring Louise Hay & Friends
(available as an online streaming video)
www.hayhouse.com/louise-movie

THE SHIFT, the movie,
starring Dr. Wayne W. Dyer
(available as an online streaming video)
www.hayhouse.com/the-shift-movie

***

Happy Days: The Guided Path from Trauma to Profound Freedom and Inner Peace, by Gabrielle Bernstein

The Prophetess: The Return of The Prophet from the Voice of The Divine Feminine, by Chelan Harkin

Transforming the Mother Wound: Sacred Practices for Healing Your Inner Wise Woman through Ritual and Grounded Spirituality, by Monika Carless

Worthy: How to Believe You Are Enough and Transform Your Life, by Jamie Kern Lima

Your Soul Had a Dream, Your Life Is It: How to Be Held by Life When It Feels Like Everything Is Falling Apart, by Rebecca Campbell

***

All of the above are available at your local bookstore, or may be ordered by contacting Hay House (see next page).

We hope you enjoyed this Hay House book. If you'd like to receive our online catalog featuring additional information on Hay House books and products, or if you'd like to find out more about the Hay Foundation, please contact:

Hay House Publishers (India) Pvt Ltd
Muskaan Complex, Plot No. 3,
B-2, Vasant Kunj, New Delhi 110 070
Phone: +91 11 41761620
www.hayhouse.co.in

—

Published in the United States by:
Hay House LLC, P.O. Box 5100, Carlsbad, CA 92018-5100
(760) 31-7695 or (800) 654-5126
www.hayhouse.com® • www.hayfoundation.org

Published in Australia by:
Hay House Australia Publishing Pty Ltd
18/36 Ralph St., Alexandria NSW 2015
Phone: +61 (02) 9669 4299
www.hayhouse.com.au

Published in the United Kingdom by:
Hay House UK Ltd
1st Floor, Crawford Corner,
91–93 Baker Street, London W1U 6QQ
Phone: +44 (0)20 3927 7290
www.hayhouse.co.uk

—

'The gateways to wisdom and knowledge are always open.'

Louise Hay